D1777968

Solid Foundations

For New Believers

Student Manual

By Nigel Brown

Parvus Magna Press
Unit 28 Hatherley Mews, London, E17 4QP
Email: sic@pmpress.co.uk
Website: www.pmpress.co.uk

© 2013 by Sharif George and Nigel Brown

Nigel Brown and Sharif George have asserted their right under the copyright, designs and patents act 1988, to be identified as authors of this work.

All rights reserved. No part of this publication (excluding the student notes sheets) may be reproduced, stored in a retrieval system, or transmitted, in any form or by any means, electronic, mechanical, photocopying, recording or otherwise, without the prior permission of the publisher or the Copyright Licensing Agency.

FIRST EDITION - MAY 2013

British Library Cataloguing in Publication Data
A catalogue record and a copy of this book are available from the British Library

ISBN: 978-1-84914-311-0

Parvus Magna Press publishes limited run and niche interest books in the UK. If you would like to see your book in print please email your manuscript to sic@pmpress.co.uk

Contents

Introduction

Welcome to your new life in Christ.

You are a Christian which means "Little Christ" and the Bible records that the followers of Christ were first called Christians in Antioch during the book of Acts

> *And when he had found him, he brought him unto Antioch. And it came to pass, that a whole year they assembled themselves with the church, and taught much people. And the disciples were called Christians first in Antioch.*
>
> *Acts 11:26*

It was intended at first as an insult but when the Christians heard this – they loved it so much they kept it as their own. Little Christs – that is our target in life that we would become like Christ.

But, in the early years after Christ we were not called Christians but "those that are in the way".

> *And desired of him letters to Damascus to the synagogues, that if he found any of this way, whether they were men or women, he might bring them bound unto Jerusalem.*
>
> *Acts 9:2*

The early Christians saw the Christian life as a journey and salvation as the entry portal into an incredible adventure which would lead, at journeys end, to the splendid glories of Heaven.

Every journey should be started with a journey plan, a set of directions where to turn and what transport methods you are going to use – for example, there is no point trying to walk to France! You have to find a way of getting over the sea.

The Bible is your guidebook, it is the instructions for the journey from here to Heaven.

Over the next several chapters we will be highlighting 10 essentials lessons which we believe will help you get through this journey.

> *Say to those who are fearful-hearted, "Be strong, do not fear! Behold, your God will come with vengeance, with the recompense of God; He will come and save you."*
>
> *Then the eyes of the blind shall be opened, and the ears of the deaf shall be unstopped. Then the lame shall leap like a deer, And the tongue of the dumb sing. For waters shall burst forth in the wilderness, and streams in the desert. The parched ground shall become a pool, and the thirsty land springs of water; in the habitation of jackals, where each lay, there shall be grass with reeds and rushes.*
>
> *A highway shall be there, and a road, and it shall be called the Highway of Holiness. The unclean shall not pass over it, but it shall be for others. Whoever walks the road, although a fool, Shall not go astray. No lion shall be there, nor shall any ravenous beast go up on it; it shall not be found there.*

> But the redeemed shall walk there, and the ransomed of the LORD shall return, and come to Zion with singing, with everlasting joy on their heads. They shall obtain joy and gladness, and sorrow and sighing shall flee away.
>
> *Isaiah 35:4-10*

1. What Went Wrong

The first lesson is all about salvation. To understand salvation we must realise how we got to the position of needing a saviour and also understand how lost we are without an intercessor.

What is it about man, which God would condescend to save him? Why on earth does man need saving and what from?

The idea of this lesson is to guide you through the salvation story so you understand what went wrong and how God rectified it.

Perfect start

> Then God said "Let Us make man in Our image, according to Our likeness; let them have dominion over the fish of the sea, over the birds of the air, and over the cattle, over all the earth and over every creeping thing that creeps on the earth."
>
> *Genesis 1:26*

And God's comment on the sixth day when he surveyed his whole creation was – "it is good". Then He rested.

> Then God saw everything that He had made, and indeed it was very good. So the evening and the morning were the sixth day.
>
> *Genesis 1:31*

The universe God created was the perfect environment to accommodate the Earth and everything was created to function in perfect order and harmony, for this was to be enjoyed by mankind

God wanted children who were like Him. He created a perfect world so that those He loved could live with Him forever.

The fall

Enter the Enemy...

The Garden was the perfect paradise but there lurked in it a sinister enemy to mankind.

Satan hates everything God loves - why is that? We know that Satan was not always evil and sinister.

> "Full of wisdom, and perfect beauty... every precious stone was your covering... you were the anointed cherub who covers... perfect in your ways from the day you were created, till iniquity was found in you."
>
> Ezekiel 28:12-19

Ezekiel gives quite a detailed picture of the beauty and wisdom of Satan when he was originally created.

All things were created good; including Satan who is also known as Lucifer, which means Bright Star.

Lucifer was full of pride and rebellion and wanted to be higher than God!

> For you have said in your heart: 'I will ascend into heaven, I will exalt my throne above the stars of God; I will also sit on the mount of the congregation on the farthest sides of the north; I will ascend above the heights of the clouds, I will be like the most High.
>
> Isaiah 14:13 -14
>
> Yet you shall be brought down to Sheol, to the lowest depths of the Pit.
>
> Isaiah 14:15

So Satan fell - actually he was thrown out of the heaven and the high position he had.

> "How you are fallen from heaven, O Lucifer, son of the morning. How you are cut down to the ground, you who weakened the nations.
>
> Isaiah 14:12
>
> And He said to them, "I saw Satan fall like lightning from heaven.
>
> Luke 10:18

The fall of man

Man had been given the ultimate gift by God - his freedom of choice, his ability to choose and this enemy, knowing that this was man's greatest strength, came to test that strength.

> Now the serpent was more cunning than any beast of the field which the Lord God had made.
>
> Genesis 3:1

Satan's approach in the Garden was to drive a wedge between God and His creation.

There was one crucial commandment that God gave to Adam and Eve and Satan targeted that freedom of choice and that single commandment.

Satan targeted their choice to obey and love.

> And the LORD God commanded the man, saying, "Of every tree of the garden you may freely eat; "but of the tree of the knowledge of good and evil you shall not eat, for in the day that you eat of it you shall surely die."
>
> Genesis 2:16-17

Not only does Satan call God a liar but he also tempts Eve with the same power he himself craved and knew he could not get.

> Then the serpent said to the woman, "You will not surely die. For God knows that in the day you eat of it your eyes will be opened, and you will be like God, knowing good and evil."
> Genesis 3:4-5

Adam and Eve broke God's commandment by eating the forbidden fruit and through this disobedience allowed a curse to separate them from God.

Did they die for it?

Yes. First they died spiritually and were separated from God and later died physically.

That is how sin works to break man's relationship with God, who is Holy.

It's more or less the same strategy as he is using now; trying to get people to doubt God's goodness, His sovereignty, His Love and His motives.

The curse

> Therefore, just as through one man sin entered the world, and death through sin, and thus death spread to all men, because all sinned.
> Romans 5:12

Mankind became separated from God and subjected to physical and spiritual death.

> Then to Adam He said, "Because you have heeded the voice of your wife, and have eaten from the tree of which I commanded you, saying, 'You shall not eat of it': "Cursed is the ground for your sake; In toil you shall eat of it All the days of your life.
>
> Genesis 3:17

Death genetically entered our bloodstream and there passed from generation to generation the trait of sin and disobedience.

Children do not have to be taught to lie or fight or cheat, they do it naturally, and it is in their nature, the bedrock of their being.

A lot of people who believe that there probably is a God often think that He's light years away and nothing to do with their real, everyday lives - separated.

Our greatest problem is not just our conduct, it is our condition, and we sin because it is our nature to sin, and we have inherited this nature from Adam.

Fallen man

So man fell and with that fall was introduced into his very nature sin. Insidious and all-pervading, it clings to the very fibre of his being and history has taught us that there is no depravity too low for man to sink to.

> *being filled with all unrighteousness, sexual immorality, wickedness, covetousness, maliciousness; full of envy, murder, strife, deceit, evil-mindedness; they are whisperers, backbiters, haters of God, violent, proud, boasters, inventors of evil things, disobedient to parents, undiscerning, untrustworthy, unloving, unforgiving, unmerciful; who, knowing the righteous judgment of God, that those who practice such things are deserving of death, not only do the same but also approve of those who practice them.*
>
> *Romans 1:29-32*

Paul when speaking to the Roman Church points out that there are none righteous - not one.

> *What then? Are we better than they? Not at all. For we have previously charged both Jews and Greeks that they are all under sin. As it is written: "there is none righteous, no, not one; there is none who understands; there is none who seeks after God. They have all turned aside; they have together become unprofitable; there is none who does good, no, not one....*
>
> *Romans 3:9-13*

Even in the psalms we find evidence of the wickedness of man.

> *They have all turned aside, they have together become corrupt; There is none who does good, No, not one.*
>
> *Psalms 14:3*

Man needed some guidance on how to be right and how to be Godly, the further away from the perfect creation he got; the quieter the voice of conscience became and the worse became his sins.

When God rescued his people from Egypt and the Egyptian gods, he took them out into the desert and he gave them the most perfect law there ever was.

The Law

The law was given through Moses and was written for him by the finger of God himself to prove it was His divine will.

The law was intended to show man the way he should go, it was not intended to replace faith but was intended as a school-teacher or shadow of what was desired.

> *For the law, having a shadow of the good things to come, and not the very image of the things, can never with these same sacrifices, which they offer continually year by year, make those who approach perfect.*
>
> *Hebrews 10:1*

It was not intended to be the final arbiter, the route of repentance was always open to them.

> *Cast away from you all the transgressions which you have committed, and get yourselves a new heart and a new spirit. For why should you die, O house of Israel? For I have no pleasure in the death of one who dies," says the Lord GOD. "Therefore turn and live!"*
>
> *Ezekiel 18:31-32*

The law was intended to show man his inability to right and his need of a saviour. It was the school teacher.

Turn and Live is an excellent definition of repentance. Repentance means to turn 180 degrees or to face the other way.

> *Therefore the law was our tutor to bring us to Christ, that we might be justified by faith.*
>
> *Galatians 3:24*

And it was always intended that faith would be paramount

> *"Behold the proud, His soul is not upright in him; But the just shall live by his faith.*
>
> *Habakkuk 2:4*

Faith is hearing what God says and doing it in spite of what your flesh desires you to do. Faith is taking God at His Word.

The wages of Sin

The wages of sin are recorded throughout the law. As you read through the law it is almost startling how many things were capital offences.

There are hundreds of scriptures that simply state the wages of sin is death.

> But of the tree of the knowledge of good and evil you shall not eat, for in the day that you eat of it you shall surely die
>
> *Genesis 2:17*

The New Testament records that the wages of sin is death.

> For the wages of sin is death, but the gift of God is eternal life in Christ Jesus our Lord.
>
> *Romans 6:23*
>
> "Behold, all souls are Mine; The soul of the father as well as the soul of the son is Mine; The soul who sins shall die.
>
> *Ezekiel 18:4*

None righteous

Sin is inherited, it is passed down the line and there are none at all who live up to the standard as described by The Bible.

> As it is written: "there is none righteous, no, not one;
>
> *Romans 3:10*

But this is not limited to the New Testament, even David saw this when he wrote.

> *Every one of them has turned aside; they have together become corrupt; there is none who does good, No, not one.*
>
> *Psalms 53:3*

The Pharisees prided themselves on their obedience to the law but Jesus went further than the Pharisees and drew out the very essence of what the law was.

He gave the law and then explained what it meant and with His explanations it is clear to see that we have all fallen short of the Glory of God.

> *"You have heard that it was said to those of old, 'YOU SHALL NOT MURDER, and whoever murders will be in danger of the judgment.'*
> *But I say to you that whoever is angry with his brother without a cause shall be in danger of the judgment. And whoever says to his brother, 'Raca!' shall be in danger of the council. But whoever says, 'You fool!' shall be in danger of hell fire.*
>
> *Matthew 5:21-22*

In the Revelation of John we have a list of people who will not inherit the Kingdom but will go to Hell.

> *But the cowardly, unbelieving, abominable, murderers, sexually immoral, sorcerers, idolaters, and all liars shall have their part in the lake which burns with fire and brimstone, which is the second death."*
>
> *Revelation 21:8*

We know that God can search out sin and destroy it.

> *"For His eyes are on the ways of man, and He sees all his steps. There is no darkness nor shadow of death where the workers of iniquity may hide themselves.*
>
> *Job 34:21-22*

We are without hope if we are in sin, the law is there to teach us that we are sinful and cannot get to God by our own righteousness.

God's Salvation through Jesus

In the beginning it was intended that man would live eternally with God in the garden of Eden but through Adam's act of sin he introduced man to mortality that is man became 'doomed to death' and we have inherited through Adams blood the curse of death.

> *Therefore, just as through one man sin entered the world, and death through sin, and thus death spread to all men, because all sinned*
>
> *Romans 5:12*

We are not sinners because we sin, but we sin because we are sinners.

We needed a plan of salvation that was sufficient to bridge the vast gap between these two infinite extremes. Man's sinfulness and God's holiness.

God's Plan - Jesus

God ordained the shedding of blood for the remission of sins.

In the Old Testament law if you committed a sin then you were required to bring a sacrifice and as the sacrifice was killed, your sins were imputed to it.

> *Also for Adam and his wife the LORD God made tunics of skin, and clothed them.*
> *Genesis 3:21*
>
> *And according to the law almost all things are purified with blood, and without shedding of blood there is no remission.*
> *Hebrews 9:22*

> *G859 – ἄφεσις – aphesis – remission freedom; (figuratively) pardon: - deliverance, forgiveness, liberty, remission.*

God was willing to accept an animal sacrifice to pay the penalty of the sins of man rather than take man's blood and life.

> *The priest shall take some of the blood of the sin offering with his finger, put it on the horns of the altar of burnt offering, and pour its blood at the base of the altar of burnt offering.*
> *Leviticus 4:25*

But the blood of bulls and rams was never enough; the children of Israel had to continually offer these sacrifices before God as they were continually unable to keep the law.

> *For the law, having a shadow of the good things to come, and not the very image of the things, can never with these same sacrifices, which they offer continually year by year, make those who approach perfect. For then would they not have ceased to be offered? For the worshipers, once purified, would have had no more consciousness of sins.*
>
> Hebrews 10:1-2

God's plan was to pay for our sin once and for all with a perfect sin offering that DID have the power to cover all sins.

> *'For God so loved the world that He gave His only begotten son, that whoever believes in Him should not perish but have everlasting life.*
>
> John 3:16

At the heart of God's plan of salvation is the function of a mediator; one who can go between a Holy God and a helpless and sinful man.

> *For there is one God and one Mediator between God and men, the Man Christ Jesus,*
>
> 1 Timothy 2:5

To be a mediator for God, He must be God and to represent mankind he must be man.

> *And the Word became flesh and dwelt among us, and we beheld His glory, the glory as of the only begotten of the Father, full of grace and truth.*
>
> *John 1:14*

So Jesus became a man and dwelt amongst us. Here he was tempted as we are tempted and suffered even as we suffer.

> *Inasmuch then as the children have partaken of flesh and blood, He Himself likewise shared in the same, that through death He might destroy him who had the power of death, that is, the devil, and release those who through fear of death were all their lifetime subject to bondage.*
>
> *Hebrews 2:14-17*

Jesus and the Cross

Jesus partook of flesh and blood in order that he might die

> *Jesus answered, 'Most assuredly, I say to you, unless one is born of water and the Spirit, he cannot enter the kingdom of God Christ came into this world for the express purpose of giving himself a ransom for our sins.*
>
> *1 John 3:5*

> "just as the Son of Man did not come to be served, but to serve, and to give His life a ransom for many."
>
> Matthew 20:28
>
> "He then would have had to suffer often since the foundation of the world; but now, once at the end of the ages, He has appeared to put away sin by the sacrifice of Himself.
>
> Hebrews 9:26

The only basis, which a Holy God could forgive the sin of man, was by His Son bearing the penalty of the sinner's guilt. Jesus paid the price for our sins by dying. The penalty is fully paid.

> For He made Him who knew no sin to be sin for us, that we might become the righteousness of God in Him.
>
> 2 Corinthians 5:21

Justice has been met, Satan can't complain. It is the perfect answer. God has not just ignored man's disobedience and sin, but has made a way where sin can be utterly cancelled and therefore man can enter his presence as if he never sinned.

> Therefore, having been justified by faith, we have peace with God through our Lord Jesus Christ,
>
> Romans 5:1

> *For the death that He died, He died to sin once for all; but the life that He lives, He lives to God.*
>
> *Romans 6:10*

Our hope

Jesus Christ not only died but rose again from the dead. Death was completely defeated and the sacrifice complete and acceptable. It fulfilled all the legal requirements of the law.

> *Moreover, brethren, I declare to you the gospel which I preached to you, which also you received and in which you stand, by which also you are saved, if you hold fast that word which I preached to you--unless you believed in vain.*
>
> *For I delivered to you first of all that which I also received: that Christ died for our sins according to the Scriptures, and that He was buried, and that He rose again the third day according to the Scriptures,*
>
> *1 Corinthians 15:1-4*

The tomb is empty and this is our hope, that even as Christ died and rose again from the dead, even so will we rise in the second resurrection.

Our hope is in the empty tomb, evidence that sin and death could not hold Him captive.

> *that if you confess with your mouth the Lord Jesus and believe in your heart that God has raised Him from the dead, you will be saved. For with the heart one believes unto righteousness, and with the mouth confession is made unto salvation. For the Scripture says, "WHOEVER BELIEVES ON HIM WILL NOT BE PUT TO SHAME."*
>
> *For there is no distinction between Jew and Greek, for the same Lord over all is rich to all who call upon Him. For "WHOEVER CALLS ON THE NAME OF THE LORD SHALL BE SAVED."*
> *Romans 10:9-13*

He is alive and continually mediates between us and God.

> *Therefore, just as through one man sin entered the world, and death through sin, and thus death spread to all men, because all sinned--*
> *Romans 5:12*
>
> *For I am not ashamed of the gospel of Christ, for it is the power of God to salvation for everyone who believes, for the Jew first and also for the Greek. For in it the righteousness of God is revealed from faith to faith; as it is written, "THE JUST SHALL LIVE BY FAITH."*
> *Romans 1:16-17*

There is a transaction.

Jesus has reconciled us back to God.

> *But as many as received Him, to them He gave the right to become children of God, to those who believe in His name:*
>
> *John 1:12*
>
> *Therefore, having been justified by faith, we have peace with God through our Lord Jesus Christ,*
>
> *Romans 5:1*
>
> *Much more then, having now been justified by His blood, we shall be saved from wrath through Him.*
>
> *Romans 5:9*
>
> *And not only that, but we also rejoice in God through our Lord Jesus Christ, through whom we have now received the reconciliation.*
>
> *Romans 5:11*
>
> *But the free gift is not like the offence. For if by the one man's offence many died, much more the grace of God and the gift by the grace of the one Man, Jesus Christ, abounded to many.*
>
> *Romans 5:15*

Complete forgiveness by faith and grace.

> *For by grace you have been saved through faith, and that not of yourselves; it is the gift of God, not of works, lest anyone should boast.*
>
> *Ephesians 2:8-9*

> Who forgives all your iniquities, who heals all your diseases,
>
> Psalms 103:3

> As far as the east is from the west, so far has He removed our transgressions from us.
>
> Psalms 103:12

> "No more shall every man teach his neighbour, and every man his brother, saying, 'Know the LORD, 'for they all shall know Me, from the least of them to the greatest of them, says the LORD. For I will forgive their iniquity, and their sin I will remember no more."
>
> Jeremiah 31:34

> If we confess our sins, He is faithful and just to forgive us our sins and to cleanse us from all unrighteousness.
>
> 1 John 1:9

The message of the New Testament is a message of God's perfect mercy and forgiveness for you and I. Jesus has satisfied Gods judgement for sin, we can't and will never be able to satisfy it.

No wonder scripture records this as "So great a salvation"

Recommended Reading

The Bible in the light of Our Redemption – E. W. Kenyon
More than a Carpenter – Josh McDowell

Romans' Road

Romans 3:10 As it is written: "There Is None Righteous, No, Not One;"

Romans 3:23 for all have sinned and fall short of the glory of God,

Romans 5:12 Therefore, just as through one man sin entered the world, and death through sin, and thus death spread to all men, because all sinned-

Romans 5:8 But God demonstrates His own love toward us, in that while we were still sinners, Christ died for us.

Romans 6:23 For the wages of sin is death, but the gift of God is eternal life in Christ Jesus our Lord.

Romans 10:9-13 that if you confess with your mouth the Lord Jesus and believe in your heart that God has raised Him from the dead, you will be saved.
10 For with the heart one believes unto righteousness, and with the mouth confession is made unto salvation.
11 For the Scripture says, "WHOEVER BELIEVES ON HIM WILL NOT BE PUT TO SHAME."
12 For there is no distinction between Jew and Greek, for the same Lord over all is rich to all who call upon Him.
13 For "WHOEVER CALLS ON THE NAME OF THE LORD SHALL BE SAVED."

2. Funeral Service for the Old Man

In this section we are going to discuss the subject of baptism. We are going to touch on what it is, what it isn't and what it means to the believer.

The core ideas in this lesson are:-

Baptism is for saved consenting adults, it is full immersion in water and although it is not salvation it is a critical event in the Christian's walk with God.

What is Baptism

Not infant

There are a number of Christian organisations that carry out infant baptism but we find no real evidence for it in the word of God.

Churches like the Roman Catholic, United Reformed, Anglican and Orthodox churches (eastern and western) all practice infant baptism as do Methodists and Presbyterians.

The idea of infant baptism is usually based on interpreting Acts 2:39 to say that children are included.

> *For the promise is to you and to your children, and to all who are afar off, as many as the Lord our God will call."*
>
> *Acts 2:39*

And also usually includes a reference to the story in Acts 16 where Lydia and "her whole household" get baptised.

These are both very tenuous interpretations of scripture. In the first, Peter is referring to the "promise" of salvation and not the act of baptism.

A clearer reading would be:

> Then Peter said to them, "Repent, and let every one of you be baptized in the name of Jesus Christ for the remission of sins; and you shall receive the gift of the Holy Spirit."
>
> For the promise [of salvation] is to you and to [the generations] your children [descendants], and to all who are afar off [ages to come], as many as the Lord our God will call."
>
> Acts 2:38-39 [added]

With Lydia and her household, this could simply relate to everyone in her household – i.e. all adults who lived with her including servants.   But it is worth noting that before the baptism of her house there came a confession of salvation.

Every single baptismal reference we will read through this study relates to adult baptism and to a time after the individuals confession of faith or salvation.

Qualifications?!

There are no qualifications or works needed to be baptised. You don't have to be perfect to be baptised – just willing.

The only qualifications are

- Faith – You believe in God, the Holy Spirit and In Jesus Christ, you believe Jesus died for your sin.

- Repentance – that does not mean you are perfect, just that you are seeking to be

- Willing – you want to do it.

> Now as they went down the road, they came to some water. And the eunuch said, "See, here is water. What hinders me from being baptized?" Then Philip said, "If you believe with all your heart, you may." And he answered and said, "I believe that Jesus Christ is the Son of God." So he commanded the chariot to stand still. And both Philip and the eunuch went down into the water, and he baptized him.
>
> Acts 8:36-38

In fact look at this scripture, "what hinders me" and Philip's answer "if you believe . . . You may" sums up the whole of the qualification. You must be a believer.

Full immersion vs. sprinkle

Acts 8:36-38 has a lot in it on the subject of baptism. Why stop to find a river when they would have had drinking water in the chariot and both of them went down into the water.

The Greek word for baptism can be found in Strong's Concordance

> G907 – Βαπτίζω – Baptizoo – Which means "to be fully whelmed" which is a nice old English way of saying to be fully wet.

The Bible only recounts full immersion baptisms and there is never an account of sprinkling in the context of baptism.

Baptism is not salvation

Scripture is very clear on the subject, first you get saved or believe and then you get baptised. Often the two things come together but not always.

There is no scriptural support to suggest that water baptism saves from sin. It is the blood that cleanses us from all sin and by confession and repentance our sin is removed.

> If we confess our sins, He is faithful and just to forgive us our sins and to cleanse us from all unrighteousness.
>
> 1 John 1:9

Baptism is not salvation, salvation precedes baptism.

> Now when they heard this, they were cut to the heart, and said to Peter and the rest of the apostles, "Men and brethren, what shall we do?" Then Peter said to them, "Repent, and let every one of you be baptized in the name of Jesus Christ for the remission of sins; and you shall receive the gift of the Holy Spirit.
>
> Acts 2:37-38

Notice the men were convicted by the preaching and sought direction. Peter's direction was "repent and be baptised" and those that gladly received his word were baptised.

> But when they believed Philip as he preached the things concerning the kingdom of God and the name of Jesus Christ, both men and women were baptized.
>
> Acts 8:12

They believed Philip's preaching and they were immediately baptised. You see faith comes before baptised.

The biggest guarantee we have that our salvation is not through baptism is in Romans where there is no mention of baptism.

> *That if you confess with your mouth the Lord Jesus and believe in your heart that God has raised Him from the dead, you will be saved. For with the heart one believes unto righteousness, and with the mouth confession is made unto salvation.*
> *Romans 10:9-10*

What does baptism mean

The Greek word that brings us the word baptism is remarkable in that it is used extensively in the Greek translation of the Old Testament law.

Perhaps the most fascinating acts of baptism were for Gentile converts to Judaism. Around the time of Christ the Jews had adopted (purely as a custom) the baptizing of proselytes or converts seven days after their circumcision.

A series of penetrating questions made it possible to judge the real intentions of anyone who wished to become Jewish. You see here a similar idea to the Christian concept of baptism – faith first, then repentance, then action.

You would have thought that going through the ordeal of circumcision would have been proof enough of the earnestness of the convert! The convert was then 7 days after the circumcision questioned about his faith and then baptised. The rule was that the convert had to strip naked and become fully immersed into flowing water. When he came up – he was an Israelite and allowed full access to the temple.

Identification with the church

John's baptism was for adults and if we look into the manners and customs of the day, we see that baptism was a matter not entered into lightly but only after a great deal of consideration. Especially if you were a gentile!

> *And looking at Jesus as He walked, he said, "Behold the Lamb of God!"*
>
> *John 1:36*

John sees Jesus coming and identifies His message with Jesus.

> *Then Jesus came from Galilee to John at the Jordan to be baptized by him. And John tried to prevent Him, saying, "I need to be baptized by You, and are You coming to me?" But Jesus answered and said to him, "Permit it to be so now, for thus it is fitting for us to fulfil all righteousness." Then he allowed Him.*

> *When He had been baptized, Jesus came up immediately from the water; and behold, the heavens were opened to Him, and He saw the Spirit of God descending like a dove and alighting upon Him. And suddenly a voice came from heaven, saying, "This is My beloved Son, in whom I am well pleased."*
> *Matthew 3:13-17*

When John baptised in the Jordan, his message was a call to repentance. When he saw Jesus he knew that Jesus did not need baptising and tried to stop Him.

Why did Jesus get baptised by John? Jesus wanted to identify with John's message; he was setting His approval on John's words.

When we get baptised we are identifying with the church, we are identifying with the congregation and we are making a public statement – I am with Jesus.

Step of obedience

There is enough evidence in the New Testament that baptism is a requirement of Christ's.

> *Go therefore and make disciples of all the nations, baptizing them in the name of the Father and of the Son and of the Holy Spirit,*
> *Matthew 28:19*

Christ's direct commandment in the Great Commission.

Obeying God's command of baptism displays the righteousness that has been given to us by God.

All through the book of Acts the disciples are baptising people.

Of course we have Jesus' own example and we have his direct instruction, which is sufficient evidence that it is a needed step of obedience

Spiritual significance

When you come to the spiritual significance of baptism, it is worth noting again that we are not speaking about the salvation of the soul or about the cleansing of sin.

The real significance comes with the public identification of the Saint with the church, with the will of God and with the example of Christ.

> "In that day a fountain shall be opened for the house of David and for the inhabitants of Jerusalem, for sin and for uncleanness.
>
> Zechariah 13:1

Baptism is an important step of obedience to take; a catalyst in the life of the believer. This public identification tells those around them to take note – "I have changed my allegiance". Like the Jewish baptising of the proselyte, you are showing the world you have changed nationality – you were of the world – you are now of Christ.

Funeral service

Paul in the book of Romans likens the act of baptism to the funeral service.

> *What shall we say then? Shall we continue in sin that grace may abound? Certainly not! How shall we who died to sin live any longer in it? Or do you not know that as many of us as were baptized into Christ Jesus were baptized into His death?*
>
> *Therefore we were buried with Him through baptism into death, that just as Christ was raised from the dead by the glory of the Father, even so we also should walk in newness of life. For if we have been united together in the likeness of His death, certainly we also shall be in the likeness of His resurrection, knowing this, that our old man was crucified with Him, that the body of sin might be done away with, that we should no longer be slaves of sin. For he who has died has been freed from sin.*
>
> *Romans 6:1-7*

Death of Old Man

Who is this "old man" that needs burying and resurrecting? It is our sinful flesh and we are showing that we are now subjecting our old sinful flesh to the new discipline of the spirit.

When we show the death of ourselves we show the life given to us from Christ and that surely is the sole aim of the Christian – to show Christ's light to the world.

> *Likewise you also reckon yourselves to be dead indeed to sin, but alive to God in Christ Jesus our Lord.*
>
> *Romans 6:11*

Burial (burying a dead body)

When someone dies it doesn't take long before the body starts to decompose and let everyone know of its presence. The body deteriorates and in deteriorating it corrupts all that is around it.

> Buried with Him in baptism, in which you also were raised with Him through faith in the working of God, who raised Him from the dead.
>
> Colossians 2:12

Our sinful flesh is a bit like that: if we don't bury it, it keeps popping up to corrupt everything we do. The act of baptism whilst ceremonial, is also a powerful weapon in the warfare against our carnal nature and against our old man.

Resurrection

When we come up out of the water, this is a symbol of the resurrected body and the new man – the rebirth.

The Old Testament often speaks about the act of birth being the breaking of water and here we have a symbiosis of that. The old man is buried and the new raises up breaking the waters as a symbol of being born again.

The resurrection is not just about the present work, it is also about the work that is to come. It's a reminder that in the future there will be another resurrection, to eternal life.

This is also a celebration of Christ rising from the dead, a simple act mirroring that amazing resurrection and reminding everyone why it is we are saved.

Public Declaration?

The reason the proselyte was so thoroughly vetted and tested by the Jewish teachers and ministers before they were allowed to join the nation, was because they understood that every Jew wherever they were and whatever they did was a representative of the nation as a whole. They understood what it is to be chosen and what it is to be set apart.

For the Jewish teacher this conversion was not a frivolous act of self-aggrandisement. This was an important and irreversible step. They did not want imposters and mockers going through the process, they understood that not everyone who arrived to be converted was genuine and willing to undergo the rigours of Jewish life.

But the acts the proselytes went through were all intended to publicly mark them as Jews.

The Christian conversion, I am pleased to say, is somewhat easier on the converts. But it still involves this public declaration of intent.

Why not now?

There are just 3 questions you need to ask yourself in order to be baptised.

1. Do I believe that Jesus died for my sin and that he rose from the dead?
2. Have I repented of my sins, do I regret them and am I turned away from them?
3. Am I willing to be baptised and associate with Jesus and His church?

Illustration

Here is a good illustration for baptism – bring in a team football shirt and hold it up. When you wear the shirt you identify with the team on the shirt – that doesn't make you a member of the team – does it?

Would you wear the strip of another team – could you imagine a West Ham supporter wearing a Spurs outfit?

Baptism is like putting on "Christ's strip" it shows the world which team you support, what side you are on.

Recommended Reading

Explaining Water Baptism – David Pawson
Foundations of Faith – Derek Prince

3. Spiritual Warfare

This is a discussion about our adversaries how we overcome them; we will be taking the lessons we have been learning over the last several weeks and applying them to our daily lives.

We overcome our adversary – the Devil – through applying these weapons – Prayer, the Word of God, Church and the Holy Spirit.

"More than heroes"

When you become a Christian you joined an army, you entered into the battleground for your soul and like all warfare, intelligence about your enemy and about his plans is vital to your survival and eventual victory.

Make no mistake, victory is already yours, it needs only to be claimed.

Our enemy – Satan, Old Nick, The Devil – whatever you want to call him is a dangerous enemy, he has many strategies at his disposal to cause the saint to stumble and fall and many strategies for keeping them fallen.

The Devil may have better tricks, but we have better weapons.

We are not born heroes, but we are Born Again as Heroes of the faith and Jesus has given us the power, through the Holy Spirit to overcome anything the wily one throws against us.

Make no mistake, we win, there is nothing Satan can do to stop that.

Two battlegrounds

All battles have a battleground where the combatants fight, and for spiritual warfare we too have two battlegrounds in which we need to stand.

The carnal or physical realm

> *Do not love the world or the things in the world. If anyone loves the world, the love of the Father is not in him. For all that is in the world--the lust of the flesh, the lust of the eyes, and the pride of life--is not of the Father but is of the world.*
>
> *1 John 2:15-16*
>
> *And do not be conformed to this world, but be transformed by the renewing of your mind, that you may prove what is that good and acceptable and perfect will of God.*
>
> *Romans 12:2*

The battleground of our flesh or the carnal realm is the battle for the sanctity of the body of the believer.

There are many pulls on us either from our fleshly lusts or from external temptations.

Many are lost because they don't understand the importance of this battleground.

Lusts of the Flesh – carnality

The lusts of the flesh are all about what you crave, what your heart wants. Temptations of the flesh are often around physical or carnal gratification.

> *Now when the tempter came to Him, he said,*
> *"If You are the Son of God, command that*
> *these stones become bread."*
>
> *Matthew 4:3*

Jesus was 40 days in the wilderness without food or water and we can surmise that he was hungry.

The lusts of the eyes – covetousness

The lust of the eyes is about covetousness, about things that are not yours but that you desire.

> *And Lot lifted his eyes and saw all the plain of*
> *Jordan, that it was well watered everywhere*
> *(before the LORD destroyed Sodom and*
> *Gomorrah) like the garden of the LORD, like*
> *the land of Egypt as you go toward Zoar.*
>
> *Genesis 13:10*

Lot given the choice coveted the rich fertile plains of Sodom and Gomorrah, rather than making peace with his uncle.

Later on we see the tragic consequences when his wife is turned to stone because she cannot take her eyes off the object of her desire.

> *But his wife looked back behind him, and she*
> *became a pillar of salt.*
>
> *Genesis 19:26*
>
> *Remember Lot's wife.*
>
> *Luke 17:32*

The pride of life – pride

Satan tempted Jesus in this area too

> *Again, the devil took Him up on an exceedingly high mountain, and showed Him all the kingdoms of the world and their glory. And he said to Him, "All these things I will give You if You will fall down and worship me."*
>
> Matthew 4:8-9

Satan was offering Jesus a shortcut to glory; he was trying to appeal to Jesus pride – offering Jesus a shortcut missing the cross and straight to the position of Glory!

The battle of the flesh

This is a war between the two natures within us. The Holy Spirit energises the new man; the things of this world energise the old man.

You will often hear the term carnal or carnality – that means that something relates to the flesh or physical desires.

> *I say then: Walk in the Spirit, and you shall not fulfill the lust of the flesh. For the flesh lusts against the Spirit, and the Spirit against the flesh; and these are contrary to one another, so that you do not do the things that you wish.*
>
> Galatians 5:16-17

Before we got saved we mostly just gave in to sin, we did what we wanted with little or no restraint. As a Christian we know that the sins of the flesh – or carnality – has a price, both in our own lives and in the lives of others around us.

> Contrary means the opposed to, to be adverse to or to find something repugnant or repellent.

These temptations are physical but are overcome spiritually.

> For to be carnally minded is death, but to be spiritually minded is life and peace. Because the carnal mind is enmity against God; for it is not subject to the law of God, nor indeed can be.
>
> Romans 8:6-7

If you feed the flesh then the flesh wins, if you feed the spirit, the spirit wins.

How do you feed the spirit?

- Prayer
- Bible reading
- Church attendance
- Ministry

How do you feed the flesh?TV/Films

- Old friends
- Old haunts
- Internet
- Certain Places
- Other People

> "He who wants to keep his garden tidy doesn't reserve a plot for weeds
>
> Chinese Proverb

The spiritual

This is the arena of the heavenly places.

> For we do not wrestle against flesh and
> blood, but against principalities, against
> powers, against the rulers of the darkness of
> this age, against spiritual hosts of wickedness
> in the heavenly places.
>
> Ephesians 6:12

Some temptations are the result of the desires of our flesh; some though have their origin in Hell.

The devil

Belief in Satan has become unfashionable in Christian circles to a certain degree, Christian counsellors would rather look at Freud and Jung and the Psychological reasons that believe in a real Satan.

The reformed thinking describes Satan as a "personification" of evil, a character made up to represent evil and wrong-doing. I have to tell you now, Satan loves that. If he can get you as a Christian to disbelieve in him, you won't bother to look for him and of course if there is no devil there is no need for spiritual warfare.

But the Bible teaches he is real, that he has a personality, he has a strategy and he has a destiny.

> *Be sober; be vigilant; because your adversary the devil walks about like a roaring lion, seeking whom he may devour.*
>
> 1 Peter 5:8

These are powerful and descriptive words. The devil's desire is to completely and unmercifully destroy your life.

The devil is always looking for a base of operations; he is looking for a foothold or beachhead from which he can launch his attacks.

The devil does not operate from a position of superior strength or even equal strength; he seeks to gain the upper hand or leverage through strategic positioning.

He has limited power and authority and he is under subjection to the Lord Jesus and to the saints of the "Most High God"

Spiritual problems

Some issues stem from spiritual attacks, they may well be aimed at our weaknesses but they are nonetheless spiritual or demonic in their root cause.

Poverty, for example may be as a result of a wrong command of money, bad spending habits and terrible decisions. Sometimes though, even when you are doing everything right, you can't get ahead.

The root of this could be the devourer, another name for Satan, but God will rebuke the devourer for you if you ask

> *"And I will rebuke the devourer for your sakes, So that he will not destroy the fruit of your ground, Nor shall the vine fail to bear fruit for you in the field," Says the LORD of hosts;*
> *Malachi 3:11*

Demonic oppression can come in many forms from things like confusion, habits and torments.

Christians cannot be possessed by evil spirits, they are possessed by God. Christians can, however, be oppressed by evil spirits and they can be set free by God.

> *For God has not given us a spirit of fear, but of power and of love and of a sound mind.*
> *2 Timothy 1:7*

The strategies

The devil uses certain strategies to undermine our authority.

Although we win in the end, Satan is trying to be sure to take as many of us to hell with him as possible.

He is a liar, he lied to Eve in the Garden of Eden and he has lied to us ever since.

> *You are of your father the devil, and the desires of your father you want to do. He was a murderer from the beginning, and does not stand in the truth, because there is no truth in him. When he speaks a lie, he speaks from his own resources, for he is a liar and the father of it.*
>
> *John 8:44*

If Satan can get you to believe a lie, he has disarmed you. There is a weapon against this – the truth. The truth is saying what God says and not listening to Satan's lies, not giving them place.

He is the deceiver and aims at ensuring that you never see the real God or, for that matter the real Satan

> *So the great dragon was cast out, that serpent of old, called the Devil and Satan, who deceives the whole world; he was cast to the earth, and his angels were cast out with him.*
>
> *Revelation 12:9*

God accomplishes His will through truth but Satan accomplishes his purposes through ties.

His target is the mind, our thoughts. His aim is to get you to believe a lie, once you believe a lie he can lead you into sin just the same strategy he used against Adam and Eve.

Faith in God's truth leads to victory faith in Satan's lies leads to defeat.

Satan's aim is to make us ignorant of God's word and our authority.

His desire is to turn you away from the will of God; he wants you to make choices based on your own will. He wants you to live independent of God and His strength and provision.

He is the accuser Satan's full time occupation is also to bring accusation against us and our righteous standing with and before God our Father.

> Then I heard a loud voice saying in heaven, "Now salvation, and strength, and the kingdom of our God, and the power of His Christ have come, for the accuser of our brethren, who accused them before our God day and night, has been cast down.
>
> Revelation 12:10

Condemnation is a favourite game of the devil, you will often hear him whispering things like.

- If you really were a Christian...
- How can God forgive you for that...?
- God's mad at you because you are not doing enough

There is a difference between conviction and condemnation.

Conviction draws you to God for forgiveness, it is the realisation that you have done something that displeases God and the desire to get it right. Conviction will always lead to repentance – if followed up.

> *If we confess our sins, He is faithful and just to forgive us our sins and to cleanse us from all unrighteousness.*
>
> *1 John 1:9*

Condemnation on the other hand pushes us away from God and offers us no hope of reconciliation. Condemnation says you are wrong and God hates you and there is no way out.

> *There is therefore now no condemnation to those who are in Christ Jesus, who do not walk according to the flesh, but according to the Spirit.*
>
> *Romans 8:1*

Appropriating victory

Our God is a God of battle.

The Old Testament records over and over again God fighting for his people. Look at God delivering the Israelites out of Egypt, God delivering David from Goliath, Look at Samson and Joshua etc.

Our God did not suddenly become passive with his enemies. The New Testament is awash with references to the battle.

> *"Do not think that I came to bring peace on earth. I did not come to bring peace but a sword.*
>
> *Matthew 10:34*

> These will make war with the Lamb, and the Lamb will overcome them, for He is Lord of lords and King of kings; and those who are with Him are called, chosen, and faithful."
>
> Revelation 17:14

Our enemy will only respond to force. He can only be defeated through warfare. He is a spiritual adversity and therefore we need to fight him in the spiritual realm.

We have been empowered and equipped for victory.

> Behold, I give you the authority to trample on serpents and scorpions, and over all the power of the enemy, and nothing shall by any means hurt you.
>
> Luke 10:19
>
> No weapon formed against you shall prosper, And every tongue which rises against you in judgment You shall condemn. This is the heritage of the servants of the LORD, And their righteousness is from Me," Says the LORD.
>
> Isaiah 54:17
>
> For the weapons of our warfare are not carnal but mighty in God for pulling down strongholds, casting down arguments and every high thing that exalts itself against the knowledge of God, bringing every thought into captivity to the obedience of Christ,
>
> 2 Corinthians 10:4-5

We can only win by pressing the battle forward, by attacking; the only way we can lose is by quitting

> *Therefore submit to God. Resist the devil and he will flee from you.*
>
> *James 4:7*
>
> *Be sober, be vigilant; because your adversary the devil walks about like a roaring lion, seeking whom he may devour.*
>
> *Resist him, steadfast in the faith, knowing that the same sufferings are experienced by your brotherhood in the world.*
>
> *But may the God of all grace, who called us to His eternal glory by Christ Jesus, after you have suffered a while, perfect, establish, strengthen, and settle you.*
>
> *1 Peter 5:8-10*

God's promise of not being moved is linked to our resisting the devil. It is linked to our participation in spiritual warfare.

How do we fight?

So we are ready to fight, we want to fight are we equipped to fight?

> *Finally, my brethren, be strong in the Lord and in the power of His might. Put on the whole armour of God, that you may be able to stand against the wiles of the devil.*
>
> *Ephesians 6:10-11*

A soldier does not go to battle in his civilian clothes, he puts on his uniform and equipment so that he is ready to fight. Paul is giving us just that instruction here. Be ready to fight.

Sanctification – avoid sinful situations

Sanctification is being set apart for holy use. What business has a Christian going into a pub or a rave?

If the carnal man seeks gratification and we give in to it, we are living carnally; feeding the carnal man increases his appetite and increases our risk of Sin.

> *Beloved, I beg you as sojourners and pilgrims, abstain from fleshly lusts which war against the soul,*
>
> 1 Peter 2:11

Peter's advice is simple; don't set yourself up for a fall.

> *Flee sexual immorality. Every sin that a man does is outside the body, but he who commits sexual immorality sins against his own body.*
>
> 1 Corinthians 6:18

Don't just avoid sin, flee from it – run away from it – have nothing whatsoever to do with it.

Do things that bring you closer to God and not things that take you further away.

Prayer – A life in communion with God

Cultivating a life of prayer creates a taste for the presence of God and this will reduce our taste for the things of this world over time.

> *Praying always with all prayer and supplication in the Spirit, being watchful to this end with all perseverance and supplication for all the saints.*
>
> *Ephesians 6:18*

Pray without ceasing, without stopping and always for everything. Live with an attitude of dependency on the Father.

The greatest foundation stone of your Christian walk is your relationship with God.

Prayer helps against demonic oppression and brings your requests straight before the throne of God.

When Jesus was under pressure – He resorted to prayer.

> *And He said, "Abba, Father, all things are possible for You. Take this cup away from Me; nevertheless, not what I will, but what You will."*
>
> *Mark 14:36*

The words of the old time gospel song remind me

> *Oh what peace we often forfeit*
> *Oh what needless grief we bear*
> *All because we do not carry*
> *Everything to god in prayer*

God's Word – read the Bible

Get the word of God inside you, know it, understand it and let it be your guide and your lamp.

> *Your word is a lamp to my feet And a light to my path.*
>
> *Psalms 119:105*

The picture here is of a man walking in darkness and with just a lamp that lights up his next step and only his next step. Let God's word illuminate your path.

> *How sweet are Your words to my taste, Sweeter than honey to my mouth! Through Your precepts I get understanding; Therefore I hate every false way. Your word is a lamp to my feet And a light to my path.*
>
> *Psalms 119:103-105*

There is no better way to fight the lies and the deception of the Devil but with God's word.

Jesus used God's word during the temptation.

> *Now when the tempter came to Him, he said, "If You are the Son of God, command that these stones become bread." But He answered and said, "It is written, 'man shall not live by bread alone, but by every Word that proceeds from the mouth of God.'"*
>
> *Matthew 4:3-4*

This was a direct quotation from the Law

> *So He humbled you, allowed you to hunger, and fed you with manna which you did not know nor did your fathers know, that He might make you know that man shall not live by bread alone; but man lives by every word that proceeds from the mouth of the LORD.*
>
> *Deuteronomy 8:3*

Fight lies with truth, fight deception with light. Fight Satan's curses with the promises of God.

> *For all the promises of God in Him are Yes, and in Him Amen, to the glory of God through us.*
>
> *2 Corinthians 1:20*

Going to Church – forsake not the assembling

The gathering of the saints is important in our spiritual warfare, it provides a firm foundation from which we can fight.

When the roman soldier fought it was not on his own out in the middle of a field seeking personal glory, but was in a tight formation with the rest of his unit all tight packed close with overlapping shields.

That is what church should be like, the whole unit united behind overlapping shields of faith.

> *not forsaking the assembling of ourselves together, as is the manner of some, but exhorting one another, and so much the more as you see the Day approaching.*
>
> *Hebrews 10:25*

The Holy Spirit

We need supernatural help in this supernatural fight, we need an empowering to overcome and God sent us the Holy Spirit to help us.

> *And I will pray the Father, and He will give you another Helper, that He may abide with you forever-- the Spirit of truth, whom the world cannot receive, because it neither sees Him nor knows Him; but you know Him, for He dwells with you and will be in you. I will not leave you orphans; I will come to you.*
>
> *John 14:16-18*

The Holy Spirit unveils things in our mind; He opens doors and intercedes for us.

> *Likewise the Spirit also helps in our weaknesses. For we do not know what we should pray for as we ought, but the Spirit Himself makes intercession for us with groanings which cannot be uttered.*
>
> *Romans 8:26*

We don't know what to pray – but the spirit does.

Spend time with the Holy Spirit and let Him help you pray.

> *For the weapons of our warfare are not carnal but mighty in God for pulling down strongholds, casting down arguments and every high thing that exalts itself against the knowledge of God, bringing every thought into captivity to the obedience of Christ,*
>
> *2 Corinthians 10:4-5*

Recommended Reading

Strategies of Satan – Warren Wiersbe

Notes

4. The Baptism of the Holy Spirit

The aim of this study is to introduce the character and person of the Holy Spirit, to highlight His role in our live and especially to show from the scriptures:-

1. That the Baptism of the Holy Ghost is a separate experience.
2. That it is not salvation but rather empowerment for serving God.
3. That it is a promise to all believers.
4. How to be filled with the Holy Ghost.

The Trinity

God the Father, God the Son and God the Holy Spirit, these three are one, they are all God and all exist in their own right.

We first come across the idea of the "compound unity" of God in Genesis where we find the Hebrew word אלהים – Elohim which is a plural word for God. Right in the beginning of the Bible we find massive evidence for the nature of the Godhead.

The word Elohim is what is known as a compound unity, a similar grammatical construct would be "a bunch of grapes" or "a Family" whilst singular it describes a compound unit.

> In the beginning God created the heavens and the earth. The earth was without form, and void; and darkness was on the face of the deep. And the Spirit of God was hovering over the face of the waters.
>
> (Genesis 1:1-2)

But this becomes even more highlighted when we come to the creation of man where we read:-

> Then God said, "Let Us make man in Our image, according to Our likeness; let them have dominion over the fish of the sea, over the birds of the air, and over the cattle, over all the earth and over every creeping thing that creeps on the earth."
>
> (Genesis 1:26)

Note the US and the OUR in this translation.

One God three persons

Christianity is a monotheistic religion. What that means is we believe in just one God. We believe that God is three distinct and separate persons but still one God.

Various methods have been used to try and describe this including:-

> The Trinity of God is like the three states of H20. When frozen H20 is called ice and when at room temperature it is called water and when boiled away – steam. All three states of ice, water and steam are all H20.

Another popular method used to describe the Trinity of God is to use the following idea.

> I am a father to my children, a husband to my wife and a son to my mother. I am "John the father, John the husband and John the son"

None of these are perfect allegories of the Trinity or Tri-Unity of God but they serve a purpose of helping to guide us in the right direction.

Jesus baptism

One of the best places in the Bible to see the trinity of God together is at Jesus baptism.

> *When He had been baptized, Jesus came up immediately from the water; and behold, the heavens were opened to Him, and He saw the Spirit of God descending like a dove and alighting upon Him. And suddenly a voice came from heaven, saying, "This is My beloved Son, in whom I am well pleased."*
> *(Matthew 3:16-17)*

Here we see all three aspects of the Godhead together, Jesus is there being baptised, God is speaking and the Spirit is descending as a dove.

The person of the Holy Spirit

The Holy Spirit is not an "it". He is the third person of the Trinity and throughout Scripture the Holy Spirit is referred to as a person.

> *But the Helper, the Holy Spirit, whom the Father will send in My name, He will teach you all things, and bring to your remembrance all things that I said to you.*
> *John 14:26*

Notice here "He" will teach you all things and also note here we have the full Trinity of God again. Jesus is speaking and the Father is sending the Holy Spirit.

> *As they ministered to the Lord, and fasted, the Holy Spirit said, Separate me Barnabas and Saul for the work to which I have called them.*
> *Acts 13:2*

Here we have the Holy Spirit speaking.

The Role of the Holy Spirit

The Holy Spirit is the executor of the will of God. In other words He is the person appointed to carry out the provisions and directions of God's will. Without His involvement in God's plan of redemption, there would have been no redemption!

According to scripture it was the Holy Spirit that raised Jesus from the dead

> But if the Spirit of Him who raised Jesus from the dead dwells in you, He who raised Christ from the dead will also give life to your mortal bodies through His Spirit who dwells in you.
> Romans 8:11

We would be lost without the Holy Spirit's role in our salvation

> The wind blows where it wishes, and you hear the sound of it, but cannot tell where it comes from and where it goes. So is everyone who is born of the Spirit."
> John 3:8

He is also the mediator through whom we are convicted of sin, righteousness and judgement. His role in our lives is such that He tells us what is right and wrong, He is the inner voice which guides our thoughts and intentions.

> Nevertheless I tell you the truth. It is to your advantage that I go away; for if I do not go away, the Helper will not come to you; but if I depart, I will send Him to you. And when He has come, He will convict the world of sin, and of righteousness, and of judgment:
>
> John 16:7-8

Through Him we are born again or born of the spirit.

> But you are not in the flesh but in the Spirit, if indeed the Spirit of God dwells in you. Now if anyone does not have the Spirit of Christ, he is not His.
>
> Romans 8:9
>
> And because you are sons, God has sent forth the Spirit of His Son into your hearts, crying out, "Abba, Father!"
>
> Galatians 4:6

> Or do you not know that your body is the temple of the Holy Spirit who is in you, whom you have from God, and you are not your own?
>
> 1 Corinthians 6:19

The Role of the Holy Spirit is to empower the Christian to live the Christian life and to execute the will of God in the world.

The gift of the Holy Spirit

The specific "gift" of the Holy Spirit is intended to help the believer to live the Christian life; to empower him or her to

minister and work in the kingdom and to supernaturally inspire and comfort him or her in prayer.

He is our helper

Jesus sent him to help us when he went to Heaven.

> "But now I go away to Him who sent Me, and none of you asks Me, 'Where are You going?' But because I have said these things to you, sorrow has filled your heart. Nevertheless I tell you the truth. It is to your advantage that I go away; for if I do not go away, the Helper will not come to you; but if I depart, I will send Him to you.
>
> *John 16:5-7*

This role as helper is pivotal to the Christians walk with God. It is this helper that empowers us to do all that God has for us.

> And I will pray the Father, and He will give you another Helper, that He may abide with you forever-- the Spirit of truth, whom the world cannot receive, because it neither sees Him nor knows Him; but you know Him, for He dwells with you and will be in you. I will not leave you orphans; I will come to you.
>
> *John 14:16-18*

He is our guide

The Holy Spirit will guide us into truth and revelation; He will speak what He hears from the throne of God. His is the voice of prophecy.

> However, when He, the Spirit of truth, has come, He will guide you into all truth; for He will not speak on His own authority, but whatever He hears He will speak; and He will tell you things to come. He will glorify Me, for He will take of what is Mine and declare it to you. All things that the Father has are Mine. Therefore I said that He will take of Mine and declare it to you.
>
> *John 16:13-15*

He will transform us.

The Holy Spirit is transforming us into the perfect image of Christ, from glory to glory, from corrupted to incorruptible.

> But we all, with unveiled face, beholding as in a mirror the glory of the Lord, are being transformed into the same image from glory to glory, just as by the Spirit of the Lord.
>
> *2 Corinthians 3:18*

Empowerment to serve God

Jesus spent three years with the disciples training them and preparing them and yet they were not fully equipped until they had received the Holy Ghost.

The early Church felt that it was so important, they sent Peter and John to pray for the believers in Samaria.

> *Now when the apostles who were at Jerusalem heard that Samaria had received the word of God, they sent Peter and John to them, who, when they had come down, prayed for them that they might receive the Holy Spirit.*
>
> *Acts 8:14-15*

Promised to all

The Holy Spirit is a promise to all; He is a freely given gift of God to the saved believer.

When we read Jesus promise in John 16 we realise that the Holy Spirit, the Helper, is intended to for all believers.

> *Then Peter said to them, "Repent, and let every one of you be baptized in the name of Jesus Christ for the remission of sins; and you shall receive the gift of the Holy Spirit. For the promise is to you and to your children, and to all who are afar off, as many as the Lord our God will call."*
>
> *Acts 2:38-39*

This was foretold or prophesied by Joel both the nature and the extent of the promise and the result all written down hundreds of years prior to Pentecost.

> "And it shall come to pass afterward, that I will pour out My Spirit on all flesh; Your sons and your daughters shall prophesy, your old men shall dream dreams, your young men shall see vision: And also on My menservants and on My maidservants I will pour out My Spirit in those days.
>
> Joel 2:28-29

Speaking In Tongues

Jesus' promise to the disciples was that they would receive power when the Holy Spirit came upon them

> And these signs will follow those who believe: In My Name they will cast out demons; they will speak with new tongues;
>
> Mark 16:17

This promise of power was repeated when the disciples were in Jerusalem after Jesus resurrection, even though they have witnessed all this Jesus still commanded them to wait.

> But you shall receive power when the Holy Spirit has come upon you; and you shall be witnesses to Me in Jerusalem, and in all Judea and Samaria, and to the end of the earth."
>
> Acts 1:8

He wanted them to be empowered to do all these works and this empowerment was the fulfilment of several promises.

The evidence

This experience we can tell from scripture was a separate or distinct experience from the water baptism or Salvation.

> *For as yet He had fallen upon none of them.*
> *They had only been baptized in the name of*
> *the Lord Jesus. Then they laid hands on them,*
> *and they received the Holy Spirit.*
>
> *Acts 8:16-17*

In this passage the language is quite powerful – He [the Holy Spirit] had fallen [G1968 – Embraced] upon none of them.

It was obvious to Peter and John that although there were miracles and the Samaritans were quite definitely saved; there was obviously a missing dimension which they immediately passed on – The baptism of the Holy Spirit.

Glossolalia – speaking in Tongues

The phrase "Speaking in Tongues" comes from Jesus' comments as he departed in Mark.

> *And these signs will follow those who believe:*
> *In My name they will cast out demons; they*
> *will speak with new tongues;*
>
> *Mark 16:17*

The important words here are

> G2980 – λαλέω – Laleo
> This means to speak or to talk
> G2537 – καινός – Kainos
> New or Fresh
> G1100 – γλῶσσα – Glossa
> Tongue or Language

Physical Evidence of the Baptism in the Holy Spirit

The baptism of believers in the Holy Spirit is witnessed by the initial physical sign of speaking with "other tongues" as the Spirit of God gives them utterance

> *While Peter was still speaking these words, the Holy Spirit fell upon all those who heard the word. And those of the circumcision who believed were astonished, as many as came with Peter, because the gift of the Holy Spirit had been poured out on the Gentiles also. For they heard them speak with tongues and magnify God. Then Peter answered,*
>
> Acts 10:43-46

The speaking in new tongues, Glossolalia, was the evidence of the infilling of the Holy Spirit.

> *And it happened, while Apollos was at Corinth, that Paul, having passed through the upper regions, came to Ephesus. And finding some disciples he said to them, "Did you receive the Holy Spirit when you believed?" So they said to him, "We have not so much as heard whether there is a Holy Spirit." And he said to them, "Into what then were you baptized?" So they said, "Into John's baptism."*

> Then Paul said, "John indeed baptized with a baptism of repentance, saying to the people that they should believe on Him who would come after him, that is, on Christ Jesus." When they heard this, they were baptized in the name of the Lord Jesus. And when Paul had laid hands on them, the Holy Spirit came upon them, and they spoke with tongues and prophesied.
>
> *Acts 19:1-6*

Speaking to God

Speaking in tongues is speaking in a new or "unknown" tongue and that speech is not aimed at man, it is not conversational, it is a language in which we speak straight to God.

> For he who speaks in a tongue does not speak to men but to God, for no one understands him; however, in the spirit he speaks mysteries.
>
> *1 Corinthians 14:2*

It especially helps us when we get to the end of our prayer, to that place where our understanding or words are unable to describe what we want to say.

> *Likewise the Spirit also helps in our weaknesses. For we do not know what we should pray for as we ought, but the Spirit Himself makes intercession for us with groanings which cannot be uttered.*
>
> Romans 8:26

How to get filled

As you can see this is one of the Christian's most powerful tools so how do we get filled.

Just ask

The major question is how do you get filled with the Holy Spirit?

You get it through prayer by asking for it. Jesus while talking on prayer taught that if we ask God for the Holy Spirit, God will give Him to us.

> *"So I say to you, ask, and it will be given to you; seek, and you will find; knock, and it will be opened to you. For everyone who asks receives, and he who seeks finds, and to him who knocks it will be opened. If a son asks for bread from any father among you, will he give him a stone? Or if he asks for a fish, will he give him a serpent instead of a fish? Or if he asks for an egg, will he offer him a scorpion? If you then, being evil, know how to give good gifts to your children, how much more will your heavenly Father give the Holy Spirit to those who ask Him!"*
>
> Luke 11:9-13

God wants you to have this gift; it is a gift for everyone.

> *This only I want to learn from you: Did you receive the Spirit by the works of the law, or by the hearing of faith?--*
>
> *Galatians 3:2*

Receiving the gift is by Faith

> *Therefore He who supplies the Spirit to you and works miracles among you, does He do it by the works of the law, or by the hearing of faith?*
>
> *Galatians 3:5*

The Spirit supplied by faith.

> *that the blessing of Abraham might come upon the Gentiles in Christ Jesus, that we might receive the promise of the Spirit through faith.*
>
> *Galatians 3:14*

The Devil wants you to think you don't deserve to receive the Holy Spirit, He's right. We don't receive the Holy Spirit based on our "works". It is a gift of God through faith.

After we have received the gift of the Holy Spirit we must open our mouth to speak whatever the spirit gives us to speak. You may not understand what you speak but God does.

God will not come down from heaven and grab your tongue and waggle it about. You must act.

> *And they were all filled with the Holy Spirit and began to speak with other tongues, as the Spirit gave them utterance.*
>
> Acts 2:4

They spoke as the Spirit gave the words.

Recommended Reading

One God or three – Stanley Rosenthal
Pray in the Spirit – Arthur Wallis
Spiritual Power – Don Basham

5. Knocking on Heaven's Door

This study is all about prayer and praying, our aim is to encourage students to enter into a regular prayer relationship with God.

We are going to work through the Lord's Prayer and see what we can learn about the art of prayer.

The Prayer Privilege

The president of the United States has two phones on his desk, one of them, the Hotline, is only known to certain privileged people so they can get direct contact with him anytime they want.

We have a hotline straight to the throne room of God and our prayers go straight there, no receptionist to field the calls; no digital queuing system with press 1 for needs 2 for praise and 3 for worship.

This direct access to the powerhouse of God is given us because we are His; He wants to hear from us.

Have you ever met a famous or powerful person and just stood there tongue tied? For some that is the exact feeling they get when they set out to pray. For some people the very fact of addressing God Almighty is fraught with fear and trepidation.

For some though it is more about the words they use, "what can I say?", "how should I put it?" or what is right to ask for? What is not?

Prayer without ceasing

Prayer is not just confined to what we do in church, though that is important, it is not just something we do when we are gathered together – but is something we are entreated to do all the time.

> *Rejoice always, pray without ceasing, in everything give thanks; for this is the will of God in Christ Jesus for you.*
> *1 Thessalonians 5:16-18*

Prayer is relationship in depth

> *Is prayer your emergency brake or your steering wheel?*
>
> Corrie ten Boom

The only times most of us prayed before we got saved was when we were up to our necks in trouble. "Oh God help me get out of this and I will..." and as soon as we were out of trouble we had no further thought about God.

Prayer is more than just a cry for help; it is the vehicle of our relationship with God.

We cannot get to know people unless we talk to them and we are unable to know God unless we talk to Him.

> *Our relationship with God will never be deeper than our prayer life*

> *A man is no bigger than his prayer life*
>
> Arthur Wallis

> *What a man is on his knees before God, that he is – and nothing more*
>
> Murray M'Cheyne

One of the critical items of note in Jesus life was his relationship with the Father. We know that He was God's only Son yet he prayed all the more because of His relationship with God.

> *And He said, "Abba, Father, all things are possible for You. Take this cup away from Me; nevertheless, not what I will, but what You will."*
>
> Mark 14:36

If there was anyone who could have done without prayer it was Jesus the Son of God. Yet in scripture we are told that He would do nothing apart from it.

> And when He had sent the multitudes away, He went up on the mountain by Himself to pray. Now when evening came, He was alone there.
>
> Matthew 14:23

> Then Jesus came with them to a place called Gethsemane, and said to the disciples, "Sit here while I go and pray over there."
>
> Matthew 26:36

> And it happened, as He was alone praying, that His disciples joined Him, and He asked them, saying, "Who do the crowds say that I am?"
>
> Luke 9:18

> Now it came to pass, as He was praying in a certain place, when He ceased, that one of His disciples said to Him, "Lord, teach us to pray, as John also taught his disciples."

> So He said to them, "When you pray, say: Our Father in heaven, Hallowed be Your name. Your kingdom come. Your will be done On earth as it is in heaven.
>
> Luke 11:1-2

"And when you pray, you shall not be like the hypocrites. For they love to pray standing in the synagogues and on the corners of the streets, that they may be seen by men. Assuredly, I say to you, they have their reward. But you, when you pray, go into your room, and when you have shut your door, pray to your Father who is in the secret place; and your Father who sees in secret will reward you openly.

And when you pray, do not use vain repetitions as the heathen do. For they think that they will be heard for their many words. 'Therefore do not be like them. For your Father knows the things you have need of before you ask Him. In this manner, therefore, pray:

Our Father in heaven, Hallowed be Your name.
Your kingdom come.
Your will be done On earth as it is in heaven.
Give us this day our daily bread.
And forgive us our debts, As we forgive our debtors.
And do not lead us into temptation, But deliver us from the evil one.
For Yours is the kingdom and the power and the glory forever.
Amen.

Matthew 6:5-13

Jesus is giving directions and specific instructions for when we pray "In this manner, therefore, pray:"

The assumption is that you will pray the question was not if but when. Prior to these instructions Jesus gave warning about praying with vain repetition so it is obvious that this prayer was not to be simply recited.

Imagine if we said the same thing over and over to each other. Jesus is not teaching a prayer but the manner in which to pray.

The Lord's Prayer

Our father in Heaven

Prayer is primarily communication or talking with our Father in Heaven, Jesus starts the prayer with a reminder of our relationship with God – or even His relation to us.

We are not coming to the throne of God as strangers but as family.

> For you did not receive the spirit of bondage again to fear, but you received the Spirit of adoption by whom we cry out, "Abba, Father."
>
> Romans 8:15
>
> But as many as received Him, to them He gave the right to become children of God, to those who believe in His name:
>
> John 1:12

> *Behold what manner of love the Father has bestowed on us, that we should be called children of God! Therefore the world does not know us, because it did not know Him.*
> *1 John 3:1*

We have been born into the family of God. This gives us the confidence to come before Him, even in the times of our greatest weakness and failings, because he is our Father we can be assured that he will hear us sympathetically.

> *For we do not have a High Priest who cannot sympathize with our weaknesses, but was in all points tempted as we are, yet without sin.*
> *Let us therefore come boldly to the throne of grace that we may obtain mercy and find grace to help in time of need.*
> *Hebrews 4:15-16*
>
> *casting all your care upon Him, for He cares for you.*
> *1 Peter 5:7*

At the same time Jesus reminds us that God, being in heaven is all powerful to hear and help.

"Before a word of petition is offered, we should have the definite and vivid consciousness that we are talking to God and should believe that He is listening to our petition and is going to grant the thing that we ask of Him. We should look to the Holy Spirit to really lead us into the presence of God and should not be hasty in words until He has actually brought us there."

R. A. Torrey

Hallowed be your Name

The word hallowed means "kept holy" it implies reverence for someone or something.

It is important for us to remember who God is and to remember His attributes like His goodness, love, faithfulness, mercy, holiness, and righteous, that He is our strength, our healer, our banner and our peace.

A sense of reverence should enter your communication with God.

> *Enter into His gates with thanksgiving, And into His courts with praise. Be thankful to Him, and bless His name.*
>
> *Psalms 100:4*
>
> *But He gives more grace. Therefore He says: "God resists the proud, but gives grace to the humble."*
>
> *James 4:6*

We are dependent on our Heavenly Father even like young children are dependent on their earthly fathers, the language of prayer is a language of dependency, praise and worship.

Your Kingdom come

> *Your kingdom come.*
> *Your will be done on earth as it is in heaven.*
> *Matthew 6*

This is literally intercessory prayer, praying for God's will to be done on earth.

In the Greek the verbs [Come] and [Done] are placed at the beginning of these two statements for emphasis.

In other words:

"Come Kingdom of God! Be done, will of God"

God has a will and plan for your life and the lives of those around you and we can begin our prayers boldly by declaring God's promises and claiming them as our inherited right.

> *for the kingdom of God is not eating and drinking, but righteousness and peace and joy in the Holy Spirit.*
> *Romans 14:17*

The Kingdom of Heaven is where the King reigns and we are declaring that we want the King to reign here, in us.

We are praying that His will and priorities will come first that is, making ourselves available for His use to establish His Kingdom.

When we pray in this way we know that God will hear us and answer us, we are praying in the centre of His will.

> *Now this is the confidence that we have in Him, that if we ask anything according to His will, He hears us. And if we know that He hears us, whatever we ask, we know that we have the petitions that we have asked of Him.*
>
> *1 John 5:14-15*
>
> *And whatever you ask in My name, that I will do, that the Father may be glorified in the Son. If you ask anything in My name, I will do it.*
>
> *John 14:13-14*
>
> *If you then, being evil, know how to give good gifts to your children, how much more will your Father who is in heaven give good things to those who ask Him!*
> *Matthew 7:11*

Give us this day our daily bread

Remember, God is our Father and He wants to meet all our needs physical and spiritual.

> *Who forgives all your iniquities, Who heals all your diseases,*
>
> *Psalms 103:3*

This part of the prayer is teaching us that we can lift up our needs to God. We know that God already knows what we need so why do we need to lift them up?

So that we know that it was God that fulfilled the need, so that we can give Him all the Glory.

> Now if God so clothes the grass of the field, which today is, and tomorrow is thrown into the oven, will He not much more clothe you, O you of little faith?
>
> Matthew 6:30

It's not as if he wants to put barriers in the way to stop you getting what you need. Like a good Father, He desires to give to you.

> Be anxious for nothing, but in everything by prayer and supplication, with thanksgiving, let your requests be made known to God; and the peace of God, which surpasses all understanding, will guard your hearts and minds through Christ Jesus.
>
> Philippians 4:6-7

Say thank you! We should not spend our whole prayer time just asking for things, we should also take time to thank God for what he has already done – for what He has already supplied.

And forgive us our debts

> And forgive us our debts, As we forgive our debtors.
>
> Matthew 6

Do we really want God to forgive us as we forgive others?

Bad relationships are one of the key hindrances to prayer.

Jesus warns us of this, when we come to the house of God and we remember that our brother is angry with us – to leave our offering and go and be reconciled first.

> Therefore if you bring your gift to the altar, and there remember that your brother has something against you, leave your gift there before the altar, and go your way. First be reconciled to your brother, and then come and offer your gift.
>
> Matthew 5:23-24

There is also a warning for couples as well, especially for husbands to be sure that they keep their relationship with their wives right so their prayers are not hindered.

> Husbands, likewise, dwell with them with understanding, giving honour to the wife, as to the weaker vessel, and as being heirs together of the grace of life, that your prayers may not be hindered.
>
> 1 Peter 3:7

We also need to come to God with a repentant attitude – search my heart God.

> Search me, O God, and know my heart; Try me, and know my anxieties;
>
> Psalms 139:23

We need to come to God, ready to repent for any dark or hidden sin – we must want to be forgiven, we need forgiveness.

When we are in sin, we often feel there is a barrier between us and God.

It's like owing money to someone and then meeting them when you don't have the wherewithal to pay them back. It feels awkward; stilted even; it feels so bad that you may even start to avoid them on purpose.

That is exactly how unrepentant sin interferes with your relationship with God. You know you can't hide the sin from him – but you try to hide yourself.

Adam and Eve tried this in the Garden of Eden,

> And they heard the sound of the LORD God walking in the garden in the cool of the day, and Adam and his wife hid themselves from the presence of the LORD God among the trees of the garden.
>
> Genesis 3:8

A Christian who sins is not in the same position as a non-believer, because if a Christian sins they are taking their confession to their Father, it's a family matter.

Take your sin to God and ask him to forgive it, repent, it's the easiest and fastest way back into the presence of God.

And do not lead us into temptation

> And do not lead us into temptation, but deliver us from the evil one.
>
> Matthew 6

This is recognition of our own tendency to fall again, keep me God from falling, show me the traps of the enemy – let the Holy Spirit have free reign in me so that I can avoid temptation.

We have prayed for God to forgive us the sins that we have committed in the past. This is a prayer for protection for the future. Repentance births a loathing for sin and a realisation of its utter destructive power to enslave.

Regular prayer means regular contact with the Holy Spirit and a regular infilling of His power to live the Christian life.

Also we are asking God's help with the fiery darts of the enemy of our soul, Lord let me see his evil machinations and see what he is trying to do and deliver me from that path.

For yours is the kingdom

> For yours is the kingdom and the power and the glory forever.
>
> Matthew 6

At the end of our prayer is a declaration of the Kingdom of God and his sovereign control or power over everything.

> *The end of your prayer is a firm declaration of God's place in your life.I would have lost heart, unless I had believed That I would see the goodness of the LORD In the land of the living. Wait on the LORD; Be of good courage, And He shall strengthen your heart; Wait, I say, on the LORD!*
>
> *Psalms 27:13-14*
>
> *Blessed be the LORD, Because He has heard the voice of my supplications!*
> *The LORD is my strength and my shield; My heart trusted in Him, and I am helped;*
> *Therefore my heart greatly rejoices, And with my song I will praise Him.*
> *The LORD is their strength, And He is the saving refuge of His anointed.*
>
> *Psalms 28:6-8*

Some practical advice

Everyone's prayer life is different and what will work with you may not work with someone else and so if any of these ideas don't work for you don't worry, try something else.

Prayer list

Many people have a prayer list, just a list of needs that they know about and have committed to pray about regularly.

You could divide the list up when it gets too big into days of the week (or even month) and just pray through a part of it each day.

Don't get hidebound by the list though, remember the Spirit intercedes for us.

> *Likewise the Spirit also helps in our weaknesses. For we do not know what we should pray for as we ought, but the Spirit Himself makes intercession for us with groanings which cannot be uttered.*
>
> *Romans 8:26*

Prayer book

This is a book where you write down all the things you have prayed for and then write down again when the prayer was answered.

One rewarding way to use this book is as a book of remembrance, to remember all the good things God has done.

How to start

Sometimes it just takes ages to get started in prayer. There are a couple of things that hinder us from getting started.

The sound of our own voice often sounds odd or off-key to us if we are not in the habit of praying out loud. This does pass.

Where to start - I often find it best to start with saying thank you to God for all the great things that he has done, for all the good things he has done in my life. It does not take many "thank yous'" to get my faith soaring.

Sometimes there is that overwhelming pressing need, God knows, so give it to Him straight away.

How long to pray

When you first start praying the idea of an hours prayer is very daunting.

First bit of advice is pray to the need – not to the clock. When you first start praying you may well find you are all done in 10 minutes – that is not a problem.

As you pray more and more and get more involved you will find your prayer time tends to increase.

Praying in tongues

Speaking in tongues is edifying, it's good and it is communion direct with the throne of God.

However, praying in tongues should not replace praying in your native tongue and is not intended to replace praying with knowledge and intelligence.

Speaking in does not mean we disengage our brain.

Speaking in tongues is a wonderful thing and we should be able to boast like the Apostle Paul.

> I thank my God I speak with tongues more than you all;
>
> 1 Corinthians 14:19

But don't let it become a habit to pass the time.

Get in the prayer room

There is no substitute for getting into the expectant and fervent atmosphere of the prayer room. Before every service and in the mornings.

There is something about corporate prayer that can really energise your prayer life.

Recommended Reading

Practicing the Principles of Prayer – David Pawson
Prayer – E M Bounds
Pray in the Spirit – Arthur Wallis

Practical Advice

Get in the prayer-room, Be where people are praying, it is very encouraging.

When I first got saved, I could pray for everything I could possibly think of in about 5 minutes, an hour was impossible, it's not enough now.

Don't compare yourself to others, it's not a competition.

Begin with praise for all the good things God has done. Then anything you know to be His will, for example for people to be saved, for His Kingdom to come. Then your personal needs and heart issues. Forgiveness for yourself and others and spiritual protection and dominion and then close once again in worship.

Abba, Father. You don't have to pray in King James English, but pray as you would share your heart with a confidant/close friend.

---

6. Invitation to Feast

The Bible is God's conversation with man, it is the primary method of hearing from God and it is the best and easiest way to get to know His will.

We are going to be looking at the benefits and blessings of the Word of God.

The Bible is God's conversation with man and it is one of the primary methods of hearing from God and it is the best and easiest way to get to know His will.

In this study we are going to be looking at the benefits and blessings of the Word of God and how it will help us achieve our full potential as believers.

The Bible is the Christian's armour and weapon all in one; it is the foremost tool of the Christians faith and the foremost weapon against doubt.

Feasting

> But He answered and said, "It is written, 'man shall not live by bread alone, but by every word that proceeds from the mouth of God.'
> *Matthew 4:4*

The word of God provides us spiritual food, in this scripture we recognise two things happening.

Firstly, Jesus overcomes temptation using the Word of God – in this case Jesus is quoting [Deuteronomy 8:3] which is Moses recalling or reciting the events that led up to the giving of the Law. Notice that the scripture speaks to the physical and spiritual level of the temptation.

Secondly, Jesus' statement that man does not live by bread alone but by every word that proceeds out of the mouth of God introduces us to the concept of the spiritual appetite for God's word and purpose.

Jesus later uses a very similar expression when he says to the disciples

> Jesus said to them, "My food is to do the will of Him who sent Me, and to finish His work.
> *John 4:34*

Spiritual food

> *Your words were found, and I ate them, And Your word was to me the joy and rejoicing of my heart; For I am called by Your name, O LORD God of hosts.*
>
> *Jeremiah 15:16*

Jeremiah compares God's words food and his language is that of a feast, "of joy and rejoicing" the Bible will become to those who read it a source of joy and rejoicing comparable to the euphoria of a well-run feast!

Paul picks up this theme when he admonishes the Corinthian church in their Bible or scripture knowledge and reading.

> *I fed you with milk and not with solid food; for until now you were not able to receive it, and even now you are still not able;*
>
> *1 Corinthians 3:2*

But it is not just the Corinthians who are in need of a reminder; Paul also admonishes the church in the book of Hebrews about the same thing. Here though, he is speaking to a people who were once quite fervent for the word of God and now have fallen away.

> *For though by this time you ought to be teachers, you need someone to teach you again the first principles of the oracles of God; and you have come to need milk and not solid food. For everyone who partakes only of milk is unskilled in the word of righteousness, for he is a babe.*
>
> *Hebrews 5:12-13*

Blessing

> *Blessed are the undefiled in the way, who walk in the law of the LORD! Blessed are those who keep His testimonies, who seek Him with their whole heart!*
>
> *Psalms 119:1-2*

The word of God and the Law are pretty much interchangeable in this context, and here we read of a blessing to those who Walk and Keep his word.

Intimacy

The word of God is a window into His purpose and thoughts; it is a portal for knowing who He is and what He desires. The more you know about God, the more you know God and the more intimate your relationship with Him will be.

> *But grow in the grace and knowledge of our Lord and Saviour Jesus Christ. To Him be the glory both now and forever. Amen.*
>
> *2 Peter 3:18*

Grow in the KNOWLEDGE is only done through an understanding of the Word.

God's Will

How do I know what God has for me? How do I know what to pray for? What does God think about this?

> Everything in the Scriptures is God's Word. All of it is useful for teaching and helping people and for correcting them and showing them how to live. The Scriptures train God's servants to do all kinds of good deeds
>
> 2 Timothy 3:16,17
> Contemporary English Version
>
> How sweet are Your words to my taste, Sweeter than honey to my mouth! Through Your precepts I get understanding; Therefore I hate every false way. Your word is a lamp to my feet And a light to my path.
>
> Psalms 119:103-105

Psalms 119 is entirely about the word of God and the psalmist's relationship to it – the longest chapter in the Bible.

When the word of God speaks of precepts – it is talking about the law and what it written down.

When in doubt "check God's word out"

God's word provides us a plan and a guide for what he wants us to do. In fact the more you read and learn of the Bible the less confusing decisions will become

> *"It is not the things in the Bible that I don't understand that trouble me, but the things I do understand!"*
>
> *Mark Twain*

The word of God guides our attitude to work (Colossians 3:17,23,24) but stops short of recommending any particular trade or living. There is a lot of guidance as to whom a Christian should marry (1 Corinthians 7:39; 2 Corinthians 6:14) but does not point the finger and say "him" or "her".

Whilst often there may not be a specific commandment to dictate a path, often there is a general principle or general guidance on what is right.

The more you read the more you get to know the style and fashion of how God works and the better you will be able to understand those things which are from God and those that are not.

The longer and more intimately you know someone, the more you will know if something will please them – Which gifts does your mother or wife prefer, what music or musicals do they like?

Growth

The word of God is needed to grow spiritually to enhance the believers' effectiveness in their own walk with God and their effectiveness in helping others. The Word of God in you becomes a well-spring from which you can draw when you need to.

> *As new-born babes, desire the sincere milk of the word, that ye may grow thereby:*
> *1 Peter 2:2*

When Jesus was at the well with the Samaritan woman, speaking about the word of God he claimed to the disciples that he had food of which they did not know.

Understanding

The word of God increases your understanding, it increases your ability to tell God's will from within and provide a resource from which others can feed.

This includes hearing from God how to help, seeing needs in the body that you can fulfil.

> *Study to shew thyself approved unto God, a workman that needeth not to be ashamed, rightly dividing the word of truth.*
> *2 Timothy 2:15*
>
> *How sweet are thy words unto my taste! yea, sweeter than honey to my mouth! Through thy precepts I get understanding: therefore I hate every false way.*
> *Psalms 119:103-104*
>
> *Get wisdom, get understanding: forget it not; neither decline from the words of my mouth.*
> *Proverbs 4:5*

> *How much better is it to get wisdom than gold! and to get understanding rather to be chosen than silver!*
>
> Proverbs 16:16
>
> *Now ye are the body of Christ, and members in particular. And God hath set some in the church, first apostles, secondarily prophets, thirdly teachers, after that, miracles, then gifts of healings, helps, governments, diversities of tongues.*
>
> 1 Corinthians 12:27-28

Faith

We hear a lot about faith and for many this word is a mystery to them but the Bible clearly tells us what faith is.

> *Now faith is the substance of things hoped for, the evidence of things not seen. For by it the elders obtained a good report. Through faith we understand that the worlds were framed by the word of God, so that things which are seen were not made of things which do appear.*
>
> Hebrews 11:1-3

Faith is saying the same thing about your circumstances as God says.

Faith is having the audacity to take God at his word.

The more of God's word you have within you the more faith you will find.

> *Faith Definition: pistis*
>
> *Conviction of the truth of anything, belief...*
>
> *...Belief with the predominate idea of trust or confidence.*
>
> *Thayer's*

Faith is intimately tied up with the ideas of truth and trust. Faith is believing and acting on what God says in His Word and trusting that to be true.

When you feel overwhelmed by the task and feel that you cannot do it – you can remember that the Bible says that you can do all things through Christ who strengthens you. When you are outreaching and your words seem to be returning to you – you can remember that God's word does not return void without accomplishing all that he has for it.

When you are sick and in pain – you know that by His stripes you are healed.

When you feel condemned – you know that Christ died for our sins and that there is now no condemnation to those who are in Christ Jesus, who walk not after the flesh but after the spirit.

Grow by hearing

> *So then faith cometh by hearing, and hearing by the word of God.*
>
> *Romans 10:17*

From hearing or reading the word of God – want more faith, read more word.

Saying What God says

The New Testament Gospel of Christ is full of power. It is able to save people. If you get it on the inside it becomes easier to share your faith.

> *For I am not ashamed of the gospel of Christ: for it is the power of God unto salvation to everyone that believeth; to the Jew first, and also to the Greek.*
>
> Romans 1:16

It's not just about reading the Bible it is about sharing the Bible with others and it's about internalising the word of God so that it cleans up the inside.

Power

While we are on the subject of saying what God says.

> *For the word of God is quick, and powerful, and sharper than any two edged sword, piercing even to the dividing asunder of soul and spirit, and of the joints and marrow, and is a discerner of the thoughts and intents of the heart.*
>
> Hebrews 4:12

Witnessing and outreaching, street preaching and evangelism are all words that have filled us with a sense of dread – especially in the early days of our salvation.

Do you say what God says about your issues? This is not about theology, necessarily, but ask yourself:-

- What does God say about marriage?
- What does God say about wayward children?

- What does God say about suffering?
- What does God say about Sin?
- What does God say about death?

This comes back to being equipped ready to do what you need to do.

Defence

God's word is a defence to our mind and our Christian walk. Many people struggle in their mind with constant attacks from the enemy and they have nothing to defend with.

> And take the helmet of salvation, and the sword of the Spirit, which is the word of God:
> *Ephesians 6:17*

It's about having the right armour on when the attack comes.

Fiery darts

The fiery darts or temptations and challenges that come from the enemy's camp are quenched – literally soaked out so they have no hold over us.

> Above all, taking the shield of faith, wherewith ye shall be able to quench all the fiery darts of the wicked.
> *Ephesians 6:17*

The Word of God is our strongest defence and our greatest weapon in the battleground of our mind.

> As for God, his way is perfect; the word of the LORD is tried: he is a buckler to all them that trust in him.
>
> 2 Samuel 22:31

Tough questions

There are many people who will challenge your faith, challenge what you believe and why you believe it. It is important to be able to give a correct biblical answer wherever you can. If you know why you believe something, it becomes much easier to argue your case and much more convincing,

> Study to shew thyself approved unto God, a workman that needeth not to be ashamed, rightly dividing the word of truth.
>
> 2 Timothy 2:15

Whatever the question, the Bible can provide the answer.

Right thoughts

How do you know which thoughts are the right thoughts? How do you know this is God or the Devil challenging you?

> (For the weapons of our warfare are not carnal, but mighty through God to the pulling down of strong holds;) Casting down imaginations, and every high thing that exalteth itself against the knowledge of God, and bringing into captivity every thought to the obedience of Christ;
>
> 2 Corinthians 10:4-5

The ability to challenge bad thoughts and hold onto good thoughts is dependent on the fuel you fill your mind with.

Bringing every thought into captivity is a part of the circle of faith. If you feed your mind with the word of God and practice it, study it, live it. It will become a part of who you are.

If you then get challenged in any way – you have the weapon at your disposal and you can capture and eject the wrong thought and have a spiritual victory.

Sickness

The word of God is a defence against sickness in two ways. Firstly it provides a basis from which you can pray for healing – you know that Jesus said you will lay hands on the sick and they will recover for example.

But also there is a promise in the Bible about listening and reading the word of God it will actually bring health to your flesh.

My son, attend to my words; incline thine ear unto my sayings. Let them not depart from thine eyes; keep them in the midst of thine heart. For they are life unto those that find them, and health to all their flesh. Keep thy heart with all diligence; for out of it are the issues of life.

Proverbs 4:20-23

Is it any wonder that this book has been fought over for over 1500 years? Is it any wonder that the martyrs of the reformation were willing to die for it?

> "The Bible is a love letter sent by God to his people in which we can perceive the heart of God."
>
> "Ignorance of the Scriptures is ignorance of Christ."
>
> "You should receive the word of God with equal care and reverence lest the smallest word of it fall to the floor and be lost."

Recommended Reading

The Advanced Bible Course – E W Kenyon
Quick Scripture References for counselling – John Kruis

7. The Place to Be

We are going to be focusing on church attendance and involvement and looking at the reasons for the order of service and for why we do what we do.

God's desire is that the children of God will grow and mature in His service and ministry.

The more often you come to church the more opportunity you will have to minister and be ministered to.

The Church

The purpose of the church is to see the children of God grow in their faith; it is the vehicle of God's blessing and his will.

> *As you therefore have received Christ Jesus the Lord, so walk in Him, rooted and built up in Him and established in the faith, as you have been taught, abounding in it with thanksgiving.*
>
> *Colossians 2:6-7*

Rooted, built up, established; this is a picture of deep roots as opposed to shallow roots. This is what determines the strength of plant and its ability to endure and grow.

> *Blessed is the man who walks not in the counsel of the ungodly, nor stands in the path of sinners, nor sits in the seat of the scornful; But his delight is in the law of the LORD, and in His law he meditates day and night.*
>
> *He shall be like a tree Planted by the rivers of water, that brings forth its fruit in its season, whose leaf also shall not wither; and whatever he does shall prosper.*
>
> *Psalms 1:1-3*

God wants us to be planted and deeply entrenched and therefore secure He does not want us blown all around the place.

God's chosen

> *For we are God's fellow workers; you are God's field, you are God's building.*
>
> *1 Corinthians 3:9*

This scripture is a picture of Divine planting and positioning.

> *You did not choose Me, but I chose you and appointed you that you should go and bear fruit, and that your fruit should remain, that whatever you ask the Father in My name He may give you.*
>
> *John 15:16*

If you are here it is a miracle of God's positioning.

What is the Church?

When we ask that question we immediately think of a building, but it isn't.

Church is the Greek word ekklēsia which means literally 'called out ones' or 'the assembly or congregation'.

It's original meaning before being used or connected with the church meant the gathering out of citizens in a public place for deliberation about the affairs of state.

The Septuagint (Greek translation of the Hebrew) translates the word "qahal" which again comes from a root word which means "to summon" or "to call".

It is used regularly to describe "the assembly" or the "congregation" of Israel. In Hebrew sense it therefore means "God's people called together by God, in order to listen to or act for God".

> *This is not so much having been "picked out from the world" but a body of people who have been "summoned out" of their homes to come and meet with God. A call to those who would listen....*
>
> *FJ Hort*

115

> *Not forsaking the assembling of ourselves together, as is the manner of some, but exhorting one another, and so much the more as you see the Day approaching.*
> *Hebrews 10:25*

So the assembly of the body of Christ (the church) is for mutual exhortation and for collective prayer, praise and worship and to hear from the mouth of God.

Order of service:

God is God of order not chaos, look at the creation or the instructions for the tabernacle, the instructions for the sacrifices, worship and even God's command concerning the handling the ark etc.

The difference between the assembling of the church and a social or political gathering is divine order.

We are aiming for God's presence.

God is everywhere but we are aiming for a special ministering presence – God doing God's business in the hearts and lives of his people.

That is the reason why we do what we do; we are contending for the ministering presence of God to save, heal, change and redeem etc.

Praise and worship

> But You are holy, Enthroned in the praises of Israel.
>
> Psalms 22:3

God dwells or takes up His abode in the praises of His people.

> Violence shall no longer be heard in your land, neither wasting nor destruction within your borders; But you shall call your walls Salvation, and your gates Praise.
>
> Isaiah 60:18

Praise means literally prizing God, to value or understand the worth of God to prize Him, to exalt him.

> Enter into His gates with thanksgiving, And into His courts with praise. Be thankful to Him, and bless His name.
>
> Psalms 100:4

Praise sees God's dominion established in the life of the worshipper and the congregation.

The devil hates praise and worship because it establishes God's authority and presence.

> Now when they began to sing and to praise, the LORD set ambushes against the people of Ammon, Moab, and Mount Seir, who had come against Judah; and they were defeated.
>
> 2 Chronicles 20:22

We can see that praise is a spiritual strategy for victory.

> Therefore let us go forth to Him, outside the camp, bearing His reproach. For here we have no continuing city, but we seek the one to come. Therefore by Him let us continually offer the sacrifice of praise to God, that is, the fruit of our lips, giving thanks to His name.
>
> Hebrews 13:13-15

Central to the idea of praise and worship is vocalising the magnificence and awesomeness of God almighty and raising His banner with our Lips.

Praise and worship are vocalised or declared, they are out loud confessions of God and His goodness. There is an element of sacrifice – it's not about what you feel or what you feel like but about who He is.

Worship is a response to the revelation of who God is.

Public prayer

Prayer as a part of the service, there is an obvious need for private prayer; that we have seen previously, but there is also a need of corporate prayer

Peter was therefore kept in prison, but constant prayer was offered to God for him by the church.

Acts 12:5

And being let go, they went to their own companions and reported all that the chief priests and elders had said to them. So when they heard that, they raised their voice to God with one accord and said: "Lord, You are God, who made heaven and earth and the sea, and all that is in them, who by the mouth of Your servant David have said:

'why did the nations rage, and the people plot vain things?
The kings of the earth took their stand, and the rulers were gathered together against the Lord and against his Christ.'

"For truly against Your holy Servant Jesus, whom You anointed, both Herod and Pontius Pilate, with the Gentiles and the people of Israel, were gathered together to do whatever Your hand and Your purpose determined before to be done.

Now, Lord, look on their threats, and grant to Your servants that with all boldness they may speak Your word, by stretching out Your hand to heal, and that signs and wonders may be done through the name of Your holy Servant Jesus." And when they had prayed, the place where they were assembled together was shaken; and they were all filled with the Holy Spirit, and they spoke the word of God with boldness.

Acts 4:23-31

Corporately they prayed specific prayers and made specific supplications, they lifted their voices in one accord.

The offering

Giving is an act of worship it is not just for paying the bills, giving is an integrated part of your worship.

> Indeed I have all and abound. I am full, having received from Epaphroditus the things sent from you, a sweet-smelling aroma, an acceptable sacrifice, well pleasing to God. And my God shall supply all your need according to His riches in glory by Christ Jesus.
>
> Philippians 4:18-19

> But this I say: He who sows sparingly will also reap sparingly, and he who sows bountifully will also reap bountifully. So let each one give as he purposes in his heart, not grudgingly or of necessity; for God loves a cheerful giver. And God is able to make all grace abound toward you, that you, always having all sufficiency in all things, may have an abundance for every good work.
>
> 2 Corinthians 9:6-8

Yes, to meet the needs of the church and the ministry or outreach but also your giving makes room in your heart for the things of God.

Preaching

Remember this is the central part of the service; it is the whole purpose of the ekklesia.

> *For since, in the wisdom of God, the world through wisdom did not know God, it pleased God through the foolishness of the message preached to save those who believe.*
>
> *1 Corinthians 1:21*
>
> *How then shall they call on Him in whom they have not believed? And how shall they believe in Him of whom they have not heard? And how shall they hear without a preacher? And how shall they preach unless they are sent? As it is written: "how beautiful are the feet of those who preach the gospel of peace, who bring glad tidings of good things!"*
>
> *Romans 10:14-15*
>
> *"The Spirit of the Lord is upon me, because He has anointed me to preach the gospel to the poor; He has sent me to heal the broken-hearted, to proclaim liberty to the captives and recovery of sight to the blind, to set at liberty those who are oppressed;*
>
> *Luke 4:18*

The word preacher in the Greek literally means "Herald". One who is declaring a message from a King.

There are two words in the Greek that describe the Word of God. The first is the Greek word Logos that is the whole revealed purposes of God, this is the word most often used to describe God's word – The Bible.

Then there is the Greek word Rhema that is "the specific word purposely implanted". The word Rhema literally means a word spoken and is used to describe the work of the Holy Spirit in accelerating the word of God into our hearts and making it a word now.

In the sermon (Logos) God wants to bring a Rhema to your heart.

Altar call

The altar call is where we transact our covenants with God, the place of decision.

The purpose of preaching the will and word of God is not just to entertain, it's also to challenge us and to bring us to a point of decision.

> Preach the word! Be ready in season and out of season. Convince, rebuke, exhort, with all longsuffering and teaching.
> 2 Timothy 4:2

When we have heard from God we want to have the opportunity to deal with God and get it right – the altar call...

8. Culture Shock – Leader's Notes

Culture shock is all about the difference that Salvation makes to the way that we live our lives. It's about living right, the way that God intended. Somehow things don't seem the same as they did before.

Oftentimes we discover we have lost our taste for sin we have gained a taste for what is right.

In this study we are going to look at the new life and what it means to be saved, what the change of carnal tastes are and how that should affect us day to day.

Sanctification means to "set apart" or to "dedicate" or "consecrate" it is the idea that something has been separated for special use.

The new life

> As you therefore have received Christ Jesus the Lord, so walk in Him, rooted and built up in Him and established in the faith, as you have been taught, abounding in it with thanksgiving.
>
> *Colossians 2:6-7*

Our new life has created a fascination and a desire for the things of God, this is at great variance with our state before we came to Christ.

The scriptures describe this as newness of life.

> Therefore we were buried with Him through baptism into death, that just as Christ was raised from the dead by the glory of the Father, even so we also should walk in newness of life.
>
> *Romans 6:4*

Things that once seemed normal to us will gradually, or sometimes suddenly, seem odd.

We get a new perspective of things like relationships, attitudes, actions and appetites.

> *In regard to these, they think it strange that you do not run with them in the same flood of dissipation, speaking evil of you.*
>
> *1 Peter 4:4*

Here is another reading

> *Now your former friends wonder why you have stopped running around with them, and they curse you for it.*
>
> *1 Peter 4:4 CEV*

There are going to be those who think it strange that you are not doing the things you used to do, they will question you over it.

Questions like "what happened to you?" or "What's wrong with you?"

We have been birthed into a new and living way as opposed to the old and dead way.

Citizens of a New Kingdom

> *God rescued us from the dark power of Satan and brought us into the kingdom of his dear Son,*
>
> *Colossians 1:13*

The word conveyed means to take from one place to another, to transfer, as a property or title to a property, from one person to another.

This is exactly what God has done for us.

> *And you, who once were alienated and enemies in your mind by wicked works, yet now He has reconciled*
>
> *Colossians 1:21*

We have become citizens of the Kingdom of Heaven and strangers here on earth, which is why this world's system seems so strange to us in many ways. The longer you are saved the odder the world's antics will seem to you.

A Kingdom has a King who has absolute rule. Jesus is the King of Kings and Lord of Lords he has absolute rule and authority in the Kingdom of Heaven and therefore over our lives.

Christ Jesus is the King not a politician. That means he does not seek our vote or approval, there is no "majority rule", Jesus is not worried about offending us.

A King determines the laws and customs of the Land. Our King has a whole new set of laws and customs of how life should be lived in His Kingdom.

If you go from one country to another you cannot transfer the laws, you cannot drive according to the laws of England while in France you have to adopt and obey the new country's 'laws.

Entering the New Kingdom entirely changes the way that we look at things. It changes our standards and our outlook. The effect of the New Kingdom is obvious because it is so great.

The Kingdom Charter: Beatitudes

The Beatitudes have been called "heart attitudes" and they lay out for us the attitudes and principles by which we are called to live our lives.

> "*Blessed are the poor in spirit, for theirs is the kingdom of heaven.*
>
> *Blessed are those who mourn, for they shall be comforted.*
>
> *Blessed are the meek, for they shall inherit the earth.*
>
> *Blessed are those who hunger and thirst for righteousness, for they shall be filled.*
>
> *Blessed are the merciful, for they shall obtain mercy.*
>
> *Blessed are the pure in heart, for they shall see God.*
>
> *Blessed are the peacemakers, for they shall be called sons of God.*
>
> *Blessed are those who are persecuted for righteousness' sake, for theirs is the kingdom of heaven.*
>
> Matthew 5:3-10

The Poor in Spirit

These are the humble those who are completely dependent on God. They recognise the absolute need of their life and of the world.

Poor in spirit, perhaps be understood better as "small in their own eyes", they see who they are before God and they keep a humble view.

Those who mourn:

Out of great grief comes great comfort. E.g. those who mourn and feel the grief of their sin feel the overwhelming joy of forgiveness. Grief can either take us from God or take us to Him. Those who go to Him find great comfort.

The meek:

This is not the spineless or the weak that never speak up. Meekness is strength controlled.

Jesus was obviously angry at the temple when He cast out the moneychangers yet not when Peter denied Him. Jesus knew who He was and therefore had nothing to prove. Everything was under control.

Hunger and thirst for righteousness:

We don't always get it right but what is our appetite like, do we prefer the company of the righteous, do we prefer our Bible to a novel, do we prefer church to football?

Is your appetite a consuming passion for righteousness, do you want it more than even food or drink.

Merciful:

The merciful are those that show mercy and grace to the undeserving. Does this remind you of somebody?

Part of the Lord's Prayer we covered last week refers to forgiving those who trespass against us. That is a New Kingdom principle.

Pure in heart:

What and how are you motivated?

The pure in heart are those whose actions are done with "unmixed" motives. Those who do not ask "what's in it for me" but whose good deeds are done with a pure heart.

Peacemakers:

The world doesn't value peacemakers, they idolise people like Oprah Winfrey who stir up and cause trouble. People trade off relationships when they get tough they are unable to reconcile or make peace. Marriages and relationships are abandoned rather than working things through. There is a blessing upon willingness to work through differences.

This also refers to evangelism, blessed indeed is the man who reconciles a Man to his God.

Persecuted:

The willingness to stand for what is right even in the face of persecution. Persecution is not always death threats and stone throwing. It can come in many forms from old friends and family alike. The blessing is for those that stand for God through all of that.

Sanctified: set apart

The issue here is sanctification which means to be separated or to be set apart.

> άγιάζω
> hagiazō̄
> hag-ee-ad'-zo
> to make holy, that is, (ceremonially) purify or
> consecrate; (mentally) to venerate: - hallow,
> be holy, sanctify.
>
> *Strongs Greek 37*

When Jesus said "follow me" that meant leaving something behind, separating yourself from something.

We have ample example from scripture.

> *When He had gone a little farther from there, He saw James the son of Zebedee, and John his brother, who also were in the boat mending their nets. And immediately He called them, and they left their father Zebedee in the boat with the hired servants, and went after Him.*
>
> *Mark 1:19-20*
>
> *As He passed by, He saw Levi the son of Alphaeus sitting at the tax office. And He said to him, "Follow Me." So he arose and followed Him.*
>
> *Mark 2:14*
>
> *Brethren, I do not count myself to have apprehended; but one thing I do, forgetting those things which are behind and reaching forward to those things which are ahead,*
>
> *Philippians 3:13*

Sanctification means to set apart for a holy use.

> *Therefore we also, since we are surrounded by so great a cloud of witnesses, let us lay aside every weight, and the sin which so easily ensnares us, and let us run with endurance the race that is set before us, looking unto Jesus, the author and finisher of our faith, who for the joy that was set before Him endured the cross, despising the shame, and has sat down at the right hand of the throne of God.*
>
> *Hebrews 12:1-2*

The weights referred to here are anything that hinders you or slows you down. Before a man runs a race he takes off all of the things that are likely to slow him down.

Sanctification does not mean that we are perfect, no it means that we are set aside for holy use.

> *"Before I formed you in the womb I knew you; before you were born I sanctified you; I ordained you a prophet to the nations."*
>
> *Jeremiah 1:5*

Now we know that Jeremiah was not perfect but we also know that he was set aside for holy use.

Marred vessels

Why the Potter's House?

> "Arise and go down to the potter's house, and there I will cause you to hear My words." Then I went down to the potter's house, and there he was, making something at the wheel. And the vessel that he made of clay was marred in the hand of the potter; so he made it again into another vessel, as it seemed good to the potter to make.
>
> Then the word of the LORD came to me, saying: "O house of Israel, can I not do with you as this potter?" says the LORD. "Look, as the clay is in the potter's hand, so are you in My hand, O house of Israel!
>
> *Jeremiah 18:2-6*

Jeremiah 18 speaks of how we are the clay in the hands of the Potter. We are marred vessels and God is going to turn us into vessels for His purpose.

> Now may the God of peace Himself sanctify you completely; and may your whole spirit, soul, and body be preserved blameless at the coming of our Lord Jesus Christ. He who calls you is faithful, who also will do it.
>
> *1 Thessalonians 5:23-24*

The aim of our salvation and life is for us to know Jesus and to become like Him.

> *But we all, with unveiled face, beholding as in a mirror the glory of the Lord, are being transformed into the same image from glory to glory, just as by the Spirit of the Lord.*
> *2 Corinthians 3:18*

As our desires and our choices lead us further and further away from this world they transform us into His image. We become like Christ, in our actions and in our language and in our tastes.

> *And a little later those who stood by came up and said to Peter, "Surely you also are one of them, for your speech betrays you."*
> *Matthew 26:73*

Peter is betrayed by his speech; he has been so long with Jesus that everyone knows that he is a Christian! It is obvious from every word that comes from his mouth.

We should be looking to Jesus and focusing on Him, on what he wants, rather than letting the world turn our heads away from Him.

If we live our life sanctified and set apart for Christ then we can live successfully and victoriously in the new kingdom.

How do we know?

One of the most difficult questions it seems if what is it that God wants? What is His will for us and for our lives?

> *Sanctify them by Your truth. Your word is truth.*
> *John 17:17*

Read the Bible, it tells you all about God and from it you will learn His character and His will.

> *Blessed are those who keep His testimonies, Who seek Him with the whole heart! They also do no iniquity; They walk in His ways.*
> *Psalms 119:2-3*

It is by understanding what God's word says that we understand what he desires from us. God's word is the charter by which we can live our lives and know that we are pleasing to Him

> *Your word is a lamp to my feet And a light to my path.*
> *Psalms 119:105*

9. Heavenly Investment

One of the most telling areas of the Christian walk is the area of money and generosity. The Bible has much to say of these areas.

One man said that you can tell how saved a man is by the state of his bank statement.

Mark of Salvation

Jesus spoke more directly about money than heaven and hell.

Our salvation will change our attitude towards money.

> Then Zacchaeus stood and said to the Lord, "Look, Lord, I give half of my goods to the poor; and if I have taken anything from anyone by false accusation, I restore fourfold." And Jesus said to him, "Today salvation has come to this house, because he also is a son of Abraham; for the Son of Man has come to seek and to save that which was lost."
>
> *Luke 19:8-10*

When you consider Zacchaeus response to the ministry of Christ, you see that the first thing he did was release his hold on worldly goods.

> Do not lay up for yourselves treasures on earth, where moth and rust destroy and where thieves break in and steal; 20 but lay up for yourselves treasures in heaven, where neither moth nor rust destroys and where thieves do not break in and steal. 21 For where your treasure is, there your heart will be also.
>
> *Matthew 6:19-21*

Lot, Achan, Saul, Gehazi and Judas all lost their destinies because of their attitude towards money.

In the Old Testament, the nation of Israel when they were brought from the land of Egypt, gave so much and so generously that Moses had to beg them to stop.

> *So Moses gave a commandment, and they caused it to be proclaimed throughout the camp, saying, "let neither man nor woman do any more work for the offering of the sanctuary". And the people were restricted from bringing.*
>
> *Exodus 36:6*

Preacher: God wants the Church to walk!
Congregation: Let it walk!
Preacher: God wants the Church to run!
Congregation: Let it run!
Preacher: God wants the Church to fly!
Congregation: Let it fly!
Preacher: It costs money!
Congregation: Let it walk!

Paul recalls the generosity of the Macedonian church to the church in Corinth as an example.

> *Moreover, brethren, we make known to you the grace of God bestowed on the churches of Macedonia: that in a great trial of the affliction the abundance of their joy and their deep poverty abounded in the riches of their liberality. For I bear witness that according to their ability, yes, and beyond their ability, they were freely willing*
>
> *2 Corinthians 8:1-3*

Paul says that even in their poverty their gratitude to God was overwhelming and then he goes on to suggest that the Corinthian church should also be showing this grace.

> *But as you abound in everything—in faith, in speech, in knowledge, in all diligence, and in your love for us—see that you abound in this grace also.*
>
> *2 Corinthians 8:7*

Mark of revelation

When you have a revelation of God you must change, there must be a personal response. You are unable to remain the same.

Salvation – When you see your sin as God sees it and you realize God's love this draws you to repentance.

Jacob's met with God and his name changed from Jacob to Israel, from schemer to Prince. To show that he had changed

Abraham had a revelation of God and it caused him to tithe.

What is the tithe?

Tithe comes from the Greek Dekatoo, which means 1/10th. We are talking about 10% of our increase, profit, or income.

Tithing is not a man idea but it is a principle of heaven. For hundred years before the law our father of the faith, Abraham, tithed (this is the first mention of the tithe), this is echoed by Moses as a legal obligation in the law.

The prophet Malachi speaks of the tithe

> Bring all the tithes into the storehouse, that there may be food in My house, and try Me now in this," Says the LORD of hosts, "If I will not open for you the windows of heaven And pour out for you such blessing That there will not be room enough to receive it.
>
> *Malachi 3:10*

And Jesus commends it

> Woe to you, scribes and Pharisees, hypocrites! For you pay tithe of mint and anise and cumin, and have neglected the weightier matters of the law: justice and mercy and faith. These you ought to have done, without leaving the others undone.
>
> *Matthew 23:23*

Abraham's Tithe

Abraham the Father of faith tithed in response to a revelation. Tithers are those who have received a revelation.

I)   Abraham's first revelation was

Recognition of God's hand upon his life.

The background behind the story

Lot has pitched his tent towards Sodom and is caught in the crossfire of war between the King of Sodom and other Kings.

Lot ends losing both his freedom and possession and Abraham goes to the rescue with 318 trained servant against a great army and wins, miracle victory.

> *So he brought back all the goods, and also brought back his brother Lot and his goods, as well as the women and the people.*
>
> *Genesis 14:16*

This was a time of victory celebration.

During this time of great rejoicing over the victory, out of the blue appears Melchizedek a priest of the Most High God. (Genesis 14:18-20)

As the priest spoke, Abram's heart was stirred he knew it was God speaking to him through Melchizedek. Melchizedek is described as the priest of the Most High in Hebrews.

> *Without father, without mother, without genealogy, having neither beginning of days nor end of life, but made like the Son of God, remains a priest continually.*
>
> *Hebrews 7:3*

Out of these words spoken, Abraham sits down and works out 10% and gives it.

> *Blessed be Abram of God most high.*

Melchizedek speaks out "You Abram are of God" – and God's hand is upon your life, you belong to God

Success was not the result of his own actions, it was God's hand upon his life.

We have been set apart by God.

> The Spirit Himself bears witness with our spirit
> that we are children of God,
>
> Romans 8:16

Your salvation was no accident.

> Or do you despise the riches of His goodness,
> forbearance, and longsuffering, not knowing
> that the goodness of God leads you to
> repentance?
>
> Romans 2:4

God's hand and goodness brought you to salvation.

Abraham tithed as he recognized God's hand upon His life; he recognized who He belonged to.

Money is symbolic of our lives

It is interesting that he gave 10% of his finance or his goods, not 10% of his time, 10% of his abilities, but his money.

> "Plenty of people are willing to give God
> credit, yet few are willing to give him cash."

Money is symbolic of our lives; it is the fruit of our skills, time and our energy. It represents everything that we are. When we give money we give part of us. I give this to You Lord because I belong to You.

Tithing is a statement of who you belong to.

II)   Abraham's second revelation is recognition that God is the Possessor of heaven and earth"

Tithing is recognition of Christ's Lordship over your possessions;

We are described as stewards.

> And the Lord said, "Who then is that faithful and wise steward, whom his master will make ruler over his household, to give them their portion of food in due season?
>
> Luke 12:42-43
>
> He also said to His disciples: "There was a certain rich man who had a steward, and an accusation was brought to him that this man was wasting his goods.
>
> Luke 16:1
>
> For if I do this willingly, I have a reward; but if against my will, I have been entrusted with a stewardship.
>
> 1 Corinthians 9:17

A steward is someone who is looking after something that doesn't belong to him.

We tend to lose sight of who is providing for us with the result that we are often fearful, anxious and burdened.

Tithing is the acknowledgement of who is in control.

> We can't charge after the Master because Master Charge has a hold over us!!"

Note that there is not a tithe on the manna because it is obvious where came from, but as soon as they reach the Promised Land God gives the command, because it is Human nature to forget whom the provider is. "I did this"

God is dependent on your stewardship.

God doesn't need us? Oh yes he does.

Abram gave to the priest.

> Bring all the tithes into the storehouse, that there may be food in My house,
>
> Malachi 3:10

The tithe is for Kingdom use, it is not to be given to next-door neighbours, charities etc. (maybe good and noble. Sure, as you give you are blessed but the tithe is for God's kingdom.)

God is very specific: the tithes or the first fruits are Mine

> You may not eat within your gates the tithe of your grain or your new wine or your oil, of the firstborn of your herd or your flock, of any of your offerings which you vow, of your freewill offerings, or of the heave offering of your hand.
>
> Deuteronomy 12:17-18

> *to bring the first fruits of our dough, our*
> *offerings, the fruit from all kinds of trees, the*
> *new wine and oil, to the priests, to the*
> *storerooms of the house of our God; and to*
> *bring the tithes of our land to the Levites, for*
> *the Levites should receive the tithes in all our*
> *farming communities.*
>
> *Nehemiah 10:37-38*

The tithe is that which comes right off the top and is given to God. Not after tax, rent, insurance, food, paid back loan etc.

We need to understand this because God is very clear, He want the first fruits of first crop.

God does not want the second months. God does not require us to redeem the second, third or fourth. God is interested in the firstborn.

Not just 10% belongs to God, but the first 10% of everything corn, wine, oil, orchards, flocks, nations and individuals, all the first fruits belongs to God.

> *All that open the womb are Mine, and every*
> *male firstborn among your livestock, whether*
> *ox or sheep.*
>
> *Exodus 34:19*

This means it belongs to God.

> *And all the tithe of the land, whether of the*
> *seed of the land or of the fruit of the tree, is*
> *the LORD's. It is holy to the LORD.*
>
> *Leviticus 27:30-31*

It belongs literally to God for His work and His purposes.

144

Desire to see God's work completed

In fact giving is a spectacular mark of the powerful move of God that happened in the book of Acts.

> *Now the multitude of those who believed were of one heart and one soul; neither did anyone say that any of the things he possessed was his own, but they had all things in common.*
>
> *And with great power the apostles gave witness to the resurrection of the Lord Jesus. And great grace was upon them all. Nor was there anyone among them who lacked; for all who were possessors of lands or houses sold them, and brought the proceeds of the things that were sold and laid them at the apostles' feet; and they distributed to each as anyone had need.*
>
> *And Joses, who was named Barnabas by the apostles (which is translated Son of Encouragement), a Levite of the country of Cyprus, having land, sold it, and brought the money and laid it at the apostles feet.*
>
> *Acts 4:32-37*

Here you see something amazing, people not giving "what they can afford" but everything they possess into the common pot. So no-one went without, the work of God went forward, and the ministers of God were provided for.

New Testament giving encompassed everything that they possessed, for us it means everything they had was available if it was needed.

III)   Abraham recognizes his need to worship

Abraham's third revelation is his need to worship God with his possessions.

Abram won a great victory and Melchizedek turns Abram towards God "and blessed be God most high, who has delivered your enemies into your hands."

God needs to be blessed; he needs to be given glory and credit for victory he needs to be worshipped, so Abraham tithes.

More than a financial transaction tithing honours God.

> *Honour the LORD with your possessions, And with the first fruits of all your increase; So your barns will be filled with plenty, And your vats will overflow with new wine.*
>
> *Proverbs 3:9-10*
>
> *and now, behold, I have brought the first fruits of the land which you, O LORD, have given me.' "Then you shall set it before the LORD your God, and worship before the LORD your God.*
>
> *Deuteronomy 26:10-11*

Worship – worth it

Tithing is putting God first; our natural impulse is to spend our money on worldly thing. This is OK for the world because they have not met Him; they do not realize that He is worth putting first.

Releasing God's blessing.

> *Bring all the tithes into the storehouse, that there may be food in My house, and try Me now in this," Says the LORD of hosts, "If I will not open for you the windows of heaven And pour out for you such blessing That there will not be room enough to receive it.*
>
> *Malachi 3:10*
>
> *His lord said to him, 'Well done, good and faithful servant; you were faithful over a few things, I will make you ruler over many things. Enter into the joy of your lord.'*
>
> *Matthew 25:21*
>
> *After these things the word of the LORD came to Abram in a vision, saying," Do not be afraid, Abram. I am your shield, your exceedingly great reward."*
>
> *Genesis 15:1*

By tithing we receive supernatural favour, a personal word or promise of great reward.

God's generous example

Giving is a sign of the inward working of God in your life. When we are giving the most we are being the most like God.

> 'For God so loved the world that He gave His only begotten son, that whoever believes in Him should not perish but have everlasting life.
>
> *John 3:16*

And his desire to continue to give to us.

> And my God shall supply all your needs according to His riches in glory by Christ Jesus
>
> *Philippians 4:19*

In fact God is so willing to give to us that he has set an unlimited cap on His generosity.

> Give and it shall be given unto you, good measure, pressed down, shaken together, and running over will be put into your bosom. For with the same measure that you use, it will be measured back to you.
>
> *Luke 6:38*

And when we give we should give generously and giving in itself is a gift from God–a ministry we are all be to be involved in.

> He who exhorts, in exhortation; he who gives, with liberality; he who leads, with diligence; he who shows mercy, with cheerfulness.
>
> *Romans 12:8*

Jesus excitement in the temple over the widow's mite, it is not the size of the gift that matters but the heart that gives it.

10. Fascinated by the Future

"The rapture of the saints"

Bible prophecy, especially end time prophecy, is a great source of encouragement for the believer.

Looking through the pages of the Bible and seeing all the things that have been foretold through the prophets and fulfilled in due time as examples to us of God's awesome foreknowledge, brings a sense of excitement and security to the saints of God.

When we bear in mind the weight of fulfilled prophecy, and we look to into the future in which Jesus has promised that he is coming back to get us and take us to heaven, this should give us ample reason to rejoice.

In this session we are introducing the study of the end times and we will be specifically looking at the rapture of the church as a distinct occurrence. We won't be going into the whole eschatological study.

1. The Bible contains a lot of fulfilled prophecies
2. Jesus has promised to come back and get us
3. Heaven is going to be awesome!

Bible prophecy

Unlike any other piece of religious literature, God's word boldly proclaims and predicts future events, the rise and fall of kingdoms and kings, the coming of the Messiah and the state of the world to come.

The Bible makes hundreds of incredibly accurate predictions many of which are well documented by historians, archaeologists and contemporary writers of the time.

We first want to consider the precision and the purpose of prophecy in the word of God.

God's word is unique; it is precise; it stands alone in exactness and in the scope of its predictions.

These prophecies and their fulfilment's are God's signature upon His Word.

The laws of probability rule against the possibility of 100's of prophecies happening by chance.

Fulfilled prophecies concerning Christ

Fulfilled prophecy is God's signature on His word and our guarantee that he is going to do all that he has promised to do.

Just, look at the prophecies of Christ's first coming, there are over 300 prophecies and 48 of these are incredibly specific. Let us examine a few of these:

> *Therefore the Lord Himself will give you a sign: Behold, the virgin shall conceive and bear a Son, and shall call His name Immanuel.*
> *Isaiah 7:14*

The messiah was to be born of a virgin mother.

> *"But you, Bethlehem Ephrathah, Though you are little among the thousands of Judah, Yet out of you shall come forth to Me The One to be Ruler in Israel, Whose goings forth are from of old, From everlasting."*
> *Micah 5:2*

The messiah was to be born in Bethlehem in Judea.

> *"Rejoice greatly, O daughter of Zion! Shout, O daughter of Jerusalem! Behold, your King is coming to you; He is just and having salvation, Lowly and riding on a donkey, A colt, the foal of a donkey.*
> *Zechariah 9:9*

Zechariah is predicts Christ's Triumphal Entry into Jerusalem on a donkey's foal.

> "Awake, O sword, against My Shepherd,
> Against the Man who is My Companion," Says
> the LORD of hosts. "Strike the Shepherd, and
> the sheep will be scattered; then I will turn My
> hand against the little ones.
>
> *Zechariah 13:7*

Zechariah also predicts that the disciples would desert Christ when he was arrested or "struck"

> Then I said to them, "If it is agreeable to you,
> give me my wages; and if not, refrain." So
> they weighed out for my wages thirty pieces
> of silver.
>
> *Zechariah 11:12*

Incredible, even the price that Jesus was betrayed for, 30 pieces of Silver is carefully predicted.

> And the LORD said to me, "Throw it to the
> potter"--that princely price they set on me. So
> I took the thirty pieces of silver and threw
> them into the house of the LORD for the
> potter.
>
> *Zechariah 11:13*

Zechariah even tells us what happened to the money, the purchase of the potter's field.

> I gave My back to those who struck Me, And
> My cheeks to those who plucked out the
> beard; I did not hide My face from shame
> and spitting.
>
> *Isaiah 50:6*

Jesus brutal treatment by the roman soldiers, he was struck and spat on.

> He guards all his bones; Not one of them is broken.
>
> *Psalms 34:20*

When Jesus was taken from the cross, the romans did not break His bones, as they usually did.

> They also gave me gall for my food, And for my thirst they gave me vinegar to drink.
>
> *Psalms 69:21*

When Jesus was on the cross they gave him Gall and wine vinegar to drink

> For dogs have surrounded Me; The congregation of the wicked has enclosed Me. They pierced My hands and My feet;
>
> *Psalms 22:16*

Hands and feet pierced

> They divide My garments among them, And for My clothing they cast lots.
>
> *Psalms 22:18*

So what do these fulfilled prophecies mean to us?

We know that our faith is established upon an unshakeable foundation, that God's hand is at work throughout history and nothing happens without God's knowledge.

God's track record is flawless. We can have complete certainty that future events will unfold just as past ones have.

There are many more prophecies well worth looking at. I have added a hand-out on the subject at the back of this book – please feel free to reproduce it.

Jesus promise

Whilst we have concentrated just on the prophecies fulfilled by Jesus, there are hundreds more fulfilled internally and externally to the bible text.

One of the greatest hopes of the Christian walk with God is that he is coming back to get us.

We want to look at what Jesus promised us.

The Rapture

Just as there were many scriptures about Christ's first coming, so there are many scriptures about his return.

The inevitability of His return

27% of all scripture is prophetic. On average 1 out of every 26 verses in the New Testament deals with Christ's return.

> *And if I go and prepare a place for you, I will come again and receive you to Myself; that where I am, there you may be also.*
> *John 14:3*

Jesus promised to come back for us. He has gone to prepare a place for us and once it is ready, he will come back.

> who also said, "Men of Galilee, why do you stand gazing up into heaven? This same Jesus, who was taken up from you into heaven, will so come in like manner as you saw Him go into heaven."
>
> Acts 1:11

The angels declared it at the ascension. Interesting here it declares that Christ will return in the same manner as he left!

> For the Lord Himself will descend from heaven with a shout, with the voice of an archangel, and with the trumpet of God. And the dead in Christ will rise first. Then we who are alive and remain shall be caught up together with them in the clouds to meet the Lord in the air. And thus we shall always be with the Lord.
>
> 1 Thessalonians 4:16-17

"Caught up" is the Greek word –

> G726
> ἁρπάζω
> harpazō
> Thayer Definition:
> 1) to seize, carry off by force
> 2) to seize on, claim for one's self eagerly
> 3) to snatch out or away

Literally we will be snatched away; the Latin word for harpazō is "rapere" which is where we get the English word rapture.

Rapture is the idea of overwhelming happiness or a mystical transportation.

Good News

There is a lot spoken about prophecy and the end times and sometimes it can almost get overwhelming.

We know Jesus is coming back soon we can see the signs around us but this is no reason to live in abject fear.

> Now when these things begin to happen, look up and lift up your heads, because your redemption draws near."
>
> Luke 21:28

And Paul's view on end times.

> Therefore comfort one another with these words.
>
> 1 Thessalonians 4:18

The only thing is – are you going to be ready, is your name written in the book?

> Then he said to me, "Write: 'Blessed are those who are called to the marriage supper of the Lamb!' And he said to me, 'These are the true sayings of God.'
>
> Revelation 19:9

Not a set date

Jesus records that no-one can predict when he is coming back:-

> "But of that day and hour no one knows, not even the angels of heaven, but My Father only.
>
> Matthew 24:36

The early church had a daily expectation of Christ's return, so should we.

> But the day of the Lord will come as a thief in the night, in which the heavens will pass away with a great noise, and the elements will melt with fervent heat; both the earth and the works that are in it will be burned up.
>
> 2 Peter 3:10

It doesn't matter when Jesus comes back as long as you are ready.

Heaven

As a thought, if this world and all that's in it took 6 days to complete, and Christ has been gone for over 2000 years – what a place heaven must be!

Heaven is the final resting place of the saints of God and has been described most poetically by John the Evangelist in the book of revelation.   His use of the word "Like" proves that even if we could grasp what he describes, it would be a very poor likeness.

And he carried me away in the Spirit to a great and high mountain, and showed me the great city, the holy Jerusalem, descending out of heaven from God, having the glory of God. Her light was like a most precious stone, like a jasper stone, clear as crystal.

Also she had a great and high wall with twelve gates, and twelve angels at the gates, and names written on them, which are the names of the twelve tribes of the children of Israel: three gates on the east, three gates on the north, three gates on the south, and three gates on the west.

Now the wall of the city had twelve foundations, and on them were the names of the twelve apostles of the Lamb.

And he who talked with me had a gold reed to measure the city, its gates, and its wall. The city is laid out as a square; its length is as great as its breadth. And he measured the city with the reed: twelve thousand furlongs. Its length, breadth, and height are equal. Then he measured its wall: one hundred and forty-four cubits, according to the measure of a man, that is, of an angel.

The construction of its wall was of jasper; and the city was pure gold, like clear glass. The foundations of the wall of the city were adorned with all kinds of precious stones: the first foundation was jasper, the second sapphire, the third chalcedony, the fourth emerald, the fifth sardonyx, the sixth sardius, the seventh chrysolite, the eighth beryl, the ninth topaz, the tenth chrysoprase, the eleventh jacinth, and the twelfth amethyst.

The twelve gates were twelve pearls: each individual gate was of one pearl. And the street of the city was pure gold, like transparent glass.

But I saw no temple in it, for the Lord God Almighty and the Lamb are its temple. The city had no need of the sun or of the moon to shine in it, for the glory of God illuminated it. The Lamb is its light. And the nations of those who are saved shall walk in its light, and the kings of the earth bring their glory and honour into it.

Its gates shall not be shut at all by day (there shall be no night there). And they shall bring the glory and the honour of the nations into it. But there shall by no means enter it anything that defiles, or causes an abomination or a lie, but only those who are written in the Lamb's Book of Life.

Revelation 21:10-27

What an awesome place, and not only that we spend eternity with Jesus!

One of the greatest promises we have is that we get to spend eternity with Christ in Heaven.

> And he showed me a pure river of water of life, clear as crystal, proceeding from the throne of God and of the Lamb.
>
> In the middle of its street, and on either side of the river, was the tree of life, which bore twelve fruits, each tree yielding its fruit every month. The leaves of the tree were for the healing of the nations.
>
> And there shall be no more curse, but the throne of God and of the Lamb shall be in it, and His servants shall serve Him.
>
> They shall see His face, and His name shall be on their foreheads.
>
> There shall be no night there: They need no lamp nor light of the sun, for the Lord God gives them light.
>
> And they shall reign forever and ever. Then he said to me, "These words are faithful and true." And the Lord God of the holy prophets sent His angel to show His servants the things which must shortly take place.
>
> Revelation 22:1-6

We shall be with Christ for all eternity.

Heavenly rewards

Getting to Heaven is just part of the wonder of being a Christian, when we get there God has prepared rewards for us.

> *Finally, there is laid up for me the crown of righteousness, which the Lord, the righteous Judge, will give to me on that Day, and not to me only but also to all who have loved His appearing.*
>
> 2 Timothy 4:8

Jesus mentions treasure laid up in heaven

> *"Do not lay up for yourselves treasures on earth, where moth and rust destroy and where thieves break in and steal; but lay up for yourselves treasures in heaven, where neither moth nor rust destroys and where thieves do not break in and steal.*
>
> Matthew 6:19-20

The rewards of Christian service are one of the things that motivate the believer.

> *Now he who plants and he who waters are one, and each one will receive his own reward according to his own labour.*
>
> 1 Corinthians 3:8

And this reward is going to be public at the Judgement seat of Christ

> *For we must all appear before the judgment seat of Christ, that each one may receive the things done in the body, according to what he has done, whether good or bad.*
>
> 2 Corinthians 5:10

Jesus clearly links the reward for works here on earth with His coming when he speaks to John in Revelation.

> "And behold, I am coming quickly, and My reward is with Me, to give to every one according to his work.
>
> *Revelation 22:12*

There are also crowns being rewarded in total the bible records 4 crowns

The Crown of Righteousness

This crown is for those that overcome temptation and cling onto righteousness.

> I have fought the good fight, I have finished the race, I have kept the faith. Finally, there is laid up for me the crown of righteousness, which the Lord, the righteous Judge, will give to me on that Day, and not to me only but also to all who have loved His appearing.
>
> *2 Timothy 4:7-8*

It is also for those who have been looking out for His appearing, those who have lived ready to be taken, expectant of His return

The Victor's Crown

> Do you not know that those who run in a race all run, but one receives the prize? Run in such a way that you may obtain it. And everyone who competes for the prize is temperate in all things.

> *Now they do it to obtain a perishable crown, but we for an imperishable crown. Therefore I run thus: not with uncertainty. Thus I fight: not as one who beats the air. But I discipline my body and bring it into subjection, lest, when I have preached to others, I myself should become disqualified.*
>
> *1 Corinthians 9:24-27*

This crown is for victors – for those who run the race to win, not looking back, who disciplines their life for the race before them.

This is the reward of the saint who is not willing to let anything stand in their way and is willing to sacrifice all for the service of the Great and Awesome God.

The Crown of Life

Some call this the martyr's crown as it is given to those who lose their life in the service of God.

> *Do not fear any of those things which you are about to suffer. Indeed, the devil is about to throw some of you into prison, that you may be tested, and you will have tribulation ten days. Be faithful until death, and I will give you the crown of life.*
>
> *Revelation 2:10*

James records that those who endures temptation receive this crown too so it is available to all believer and you don't necessarily have to have your head chopped off to get it.

> *Blessed is the man who endures temptation; for when he has been approved, he will receive the crown of life which the Lord has promised to those who love Him.*
>
> *James 1:12*

The Crown of Rejoicing

The soul winner's crown, it's the crown given to those who win souls.

> *For what is our hope, or joy, or crown of rejoicing? Is it not even you in the presence of our Lord Jesus Christ at His coming? For you are our glory and joy.*
>
> *1 Thessalonians 2:19-20*

This is once again a crown available to all, regardless of station and ability,

> *The fruit of the righteous is a tree of life, and he who wins souls is wise.*
>
> *Proverbs 11:30*

The Pastors Crown

There is a special reward reserved for those who shepherd the flock of God, it is for those that faithfully minister as pastors, teachers and leaders with pastoral duties like home care team leaders.

> *The elders who are among you I exhort, I who am a fellow elder and a witness of the sufferings of Christ, and also a partaker of the glory that will be revealed:*
>
> *Shepherd the flock of God which is among you, serving as overseers, not by compulsion but willingly, not for dishonest gain but eagerly; nor as being lords over those entrusted to you, but being examples to the flock; and when the Chief Shepherd appears, you will receive the crown of glory that does not fade away.*
>
> *1 Peter 5:1-4*

Finally then brethren

The evidence in the bible is overwhelming that the biggest danger to Christians is not external but internal to the church and to the saint. That we would fail to walk in a way pleasing to God and lose our rewards.

> *Finally then, brethren, we urge and exhort in the Lord Jesus that you should abound more and more, just as you received from us how you ought to walk and to please God;*
>
> *1 Thessalonians 4:1*

Now is not the time for being secret Christians but for us to be bold and uncompromising in our faith towards God.

> *not forsaking the assembling of ourselves together, as is the manner of some, but exhorting one another, and so much the more as you see the Day approaching.*
>
> *Hebrews 10:25*

To finish on Jesus words

> *Now when these things begin to happen, look up and lift up your heads, because your redemption draws near."*
>
> *Luke 21:28*

Some End Time Scriptures

We have included here some basic information about end times and some interesting scriptures.

These are not in any particular order.

Rapture of the Saints
1 Thessalonians 4:13-18, 1 Corinthians 15:51-54

Marriage Supper of the Lamb
Revelations 19:7-9

Judgement Seat of Christ
2 Corinthians 5:10, Romans 14:10, 1 Corinthians 3:10 – 15

Lake of Fire
Revelations 19:20, Revelations 20:10, 14 - 15

Christ to reign on Earth
2 Thessalonians 1:7-10, 2 Thessalonians 3:13 Colossians 3:4

2nd Coming
2 Thessalonians1:7-12, Revelations 19:11-21

Tribulation
Matthew 24:

Anti-Christ
Revelations 13:1

False Prophet
Revelations 13:11

Great Tribulation
Daniel 9:2

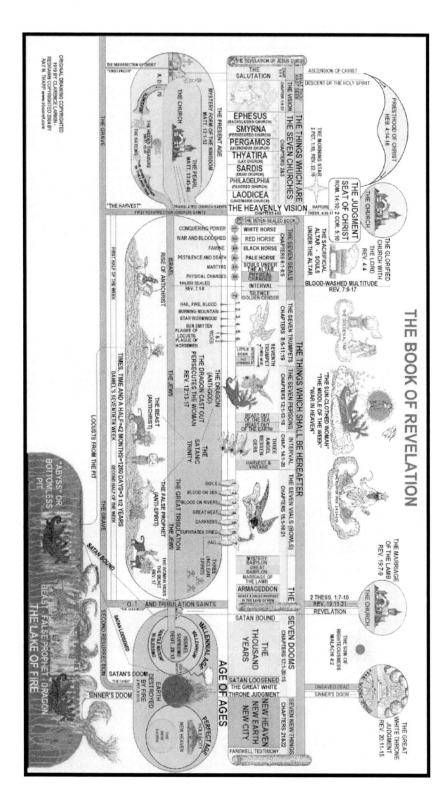

THE BOOK OF REVELATION

ORIGINAL DRAWING COPYRIGHTED
1919 BY CLARENCE LARKIN.
REPRINT COPYRIGHTED 2004 BY
RAY H. THARP www.csooo-cs.com

Glossary of Terms

Amen: Simply means "so be it", it's a word that confirms what has gone before.

Baptism: The act of being fully immersed in water – publicly declaring your new allegiance to God's kingdom. Baptism doesn't save.

Baptism of the Holy Spirit: The Baptism of the Holy Spirit, with the evidence of Speaking in tongues is a gift of God for all believers.

Christian: Is anyone who has accepted the Lord Jesus Christ as their saviour and Lord.

Church: The gathering together of the saints of God.

End Times: The time at the end of this age, just before Jesus comes back.

Forgiveness: God has forgiven us – which means he has not treated us according to what we deserve. We are called to forgive others, which means, we do not treat them as they deserve.

Hallelujah: Used in praise and it means "Praise Yahweh" or "Praise God" it's Hebrew!

Holiness: Living clean of Sin, acting and walking in obedience to the commands of God. Holiness is a result of sanctification.

Justification: The act whereby Jesus forgives our sins – Remember Just if I'd never sinned.

Meditation: To think on God's word and his goodness in quiet contemplation.

Offering: A gift to god, an act of Worship

Prayer: The act of communicating with God.

Rapture: The saints of God taken from the earth up to heaven

Redeemed: Redemption is the act of buying something back, or paying a price to return something to your possession

Resurrection: Usually referring to Jesus rising from the dead, physically and spiritually. Also what happens to the saints at the rapture.

Salvation: The act of God redeeming an individual from their sin. It is not a single event, though it often starts as such, but an ongoing work of Christ in you. Salvation happens when an individual realises that they have sinned and need a saviour and then accept Jesus into their lives.

Sanctification: Something which is set apart for Holy use. We are sanctified for the use of God.

Saved: We use this term to refer to those who have accepted Christ as their Lord and Saviour and who are living as if He is.

Scripture: The word of God, the Bible.

Sin: An act of rebellion against God, usually something that goes against the commandments in the Bible – though not exclusively so.

Speaking in Tongues: The act of Speaking in an unknown tongue to God. There are two variations on this – One is speaking in tongues to prophecy, in which case there must be an interpretation. The other is speaking in tongues in prayer, as the spirit giveth utterance.

Thanksgiving: Saying thank you to God for the things He has done for you, for His benefits (compare worship)

Tithe: An offering of 1/10th of your income before tax to God.

Trinity: The three persons who co-equally make up the Godhead. God the Father, God the Son and God the Holy Spirit. Each of them individually fully God.

Worship: The act of ascribing praise to God, either through prayer or song, thanking God for who he is.

Lightning Source UK Ltd.
Milton Keynes UK
UKOW030035240513

211153UK00006B/37/P

CS0042015 3TRP